make it with a
CAKE MIX

Recipes and Photographs by **LIZZY EARLY**

Design copyrighted 2014 by Covenant Communications, Inc.
American Fork, Utah

Copyright 2014 by Lizzy Early
Photography by Lizzy Early © 2014
Cover and book design by Christina Marcano © 2014 Covenant Communications, Inc.

All rights reserved. No part of this book may be reproduced in any format or in any medium without the written permission of the publisher, Covenant Communications, Inc., P.O. Box 416, American Fork, UT 84003. This work is not an official publication of The Church of Jesus Christ of Latter-day Saints. The views expressed within this work are the sole responsibility of the author and do not necessarily reflect the position of The Church of Jesus Christ of Latter-day Saints, Covenant Communications, Inc., or any other entity.

Printed in China
First Printing: March 2014

20 19 18 17 16 15 14   10 9 8 7 6 5 4 3 2 1

ISBN-13: 978-1-62108-701-4

LIZZY EARLY grew up in Portland, Oregon, in a family of five. She started baking when in high school and quickly became known for her way around a kitchen. A 2013 graduate of Brigham Young University in broadcast journalism, she's the proud owner of www.YourCupofCake.com—and, more than anything, she loves to teach others how to bake.

Want to connect with Lizzy?
Blog: www.YourCupofCake.com
Twitter: @LizzysCupofCake
Instagram: YourCupofCake
Facebook: facebook.com/yourcupofcake

To my **Grandma Hansen** for introducing me to the beauty of baking and the memories and stories that come with it.

And to my **Grandpa Hansen** for his love of photography and love of family.

I love you both.

TABLE OF CONTENTS

CUPCAKES: 1

BLACK FOREST CUPCAKES 3

BLACKBERRY LEMONADE CUPCAKES 4

S'MORES CUPCAKES 7

DOUBLE CHOCOLATE CUPCAKES FILLED WITH SWEET MASCARPONE 8

PINEAPPLE CREAM CUPCAKES 11

CHOCOLATE BANANA CREAM PIE CUPCAKES 12

DIRT CUPCAKES 15

CAKE BATTER CUPCAKES 16

PEPPERMINT BARK CUPCAKES 19

DOUBLE CHOCOLATE PEANUT BUTTER CUPCAKES 20

COCONUT LIME CUPCAKES................... 23

RASPBERRY WHITE CHOCOLATE MOUSSE CUPCAKES 24

SWEET POTATO PIE CUPCAKES WITH BROWN SUGAR BUTTERCREAM 27

CHOCOLATE ALMOND RASPBERRY CUPCAKES 29

MARASCHINO CHERRY CUPCAKES ... 30

BLUEBERRY CINNAMON TOAST CRUNCH™ CUPCAKES.............................. 33

STRAWBERRY RED VELVET CUPCAKES 34

BUNDT CAKES: 37

BLUEBERRY ALMOND MINI BUNDT CAKE 39

CHOCOLATE ZUCCHINI BUNDT CAKE ... 40

RASPBERRY WHITE CHOCOLATE BUNDT CAKE 43

BREAKFAST BUNDT CAKE 44

HOT CHOCOLATE BUNDT CAKE 47

BANANA BUNDT WITH CHOCOLATE GLAZE AND WALNUTS 48

LEMON ALMOND POPPY SEED BUNDT CAKE 51

DARK CHOCOLATE BUNDT CAKE 52

MINI CHERRY ALMOND BUNDTS 55

PEACHES AND CREAM BUNDT CAKE ... 56

PUMPKIN BUNDT CAKE 59

PINEAPPLE CAKE WITH SWEET STRAWBERRIES 60

BIRTHDAY BUNDT CAKE 63

CHOCOLATE STRAWBERRY BUNDT CAKE 64

RASPBERRY LEMONADE BUNDT CAKE 67

CINNAMON SWIRL BUNDT CAKE 68

ORANGE CRANBERRY BUNDT CAKE .. 71

LAYERED CAKES: 73

- ANDES MINT CAKE 75
- BIRTHDAY CAKE 76
- CHOCOLATE HAZELNUT CAKE 79
- COOKIE DOUGH CAKE 80
- HAWAIIAN VACATION CAKE 83
- CHOCOLATE MALT CAKE 84
- COOKIES AND CREAM CAKE 87
- STRAWBERRY VANILLA CAKE 88
- ROCKY ROAD CAKE 91
- BANANA PEANUT BUTTER CAKE 92
- LEMON BERRY CAKE 95
- SNICKERDOODLE CAKE 96
- LEMON RASPBERRY WHIPPED CREAM CAKE 98

COOKIES: 101

PEANUT BUTTER CHOCOLATE CHIP
PUMPKIN COOKIES..................................103

CHOCOLATE CRINKLES COOKIES.......104

BANANA SPLIT COOKIES 107

CHOCOLATE CHIP COOKIES 108

ULTIMATE GRASSHOPPER COOKIES 111

COOKIES AND CREAM COOKIES..........112

CHOCOLATE CANDY CANE COOKIES .115

SNICKERDOODLES 116

EGGNOG COOKIES...................................119

KEY LIME PIE COOKIES 120

CHOCOLATE TRAIL MIX COOKIES........123

LEMON COOKIES.....................................124

WHOOPIE PIES: 127

GERMAN CHOCOLATE WHOOPIE PIES 129
BROWNIE CREAM WHOOPIE PIES 130
RED VELVET WHOOPIE PIES 133
SNICKERDOODLE PEANUT BUTTER WHOOPIE PIES 134
PUMPKIN CHOCOLATE CHIP WHOOPIE PIES 137
OATMEAL WHOOPIE PIES 138
CARROT CAKE WHOOPIE PIES 141
CHOCOLATE COCONUT WHOOPIE PIES 142
DOUBLE CHOCOLATE PEANUT BUTTER WHOOPIE PIES 145

MORE TO CRAVE: 147

RED VELVET S'MORES BARS 149

DIRT DOUGHNUTS 150

RED VELVET PUPPY CHOW 153

CAKE BATTER BROWNIES 154

CAKE BATTER RICE CRISPY TREATS 157

DEVIL'S FOOD RICE CRISPY TREATS 158

CHOCOLATE WAFFLES 161

RED VELVET DOUGHNUTS 162

KEY LIME COOKIE BARS 165

PUMPKIN PIE BARS 166

PEANUT BUTTER SWIRL BROWNIES ... 169

APPLE CRISP 170

EASY BERRY COBBLER 173

TIPS AND TRICKS: 175

- CAKE MIX SUBSTITUTIONS 176
- BAKING TIMES 178
- CUTTING A RECIPE IN HALF 178
- TRICKS TO GETTING "ROUND" TOPS ON YOUR CUPCAKES 178
- CUPCAKE LINERS 179
- PICKING YOUR PIPING TIP 179
- HOW TO FILL A PIPING BAG 180
- FOOD SCOOPS 182
- BUTTERCREAM BASICS 183
- COMMON BUTTERCREAM MISTAKES 184
- REMOVING A BUNDT CAKE FROM THE PAN 184
- DECIDING WHICH CAKE PANS TO USE 184
- LINING YOUR PANS 185
- WHAT ABOUT "LEVELING" THE CAKES? 185
- MAKING MORE LAYERS 185
- STACKING THE CAKE 186
- FROSTING THE CAKE 186
- CUTTING THE CAKE 187
- FREQUENTLY ASKED QUESTIONS 188

INDEX: 190

Introduction

I believe that anyone can bake something beautiful and delicious. It doesn't take twenty ingredients, it doesn't take three hours, it doesn't take years at pastry school, and you don't have to own a fancy rotating cake stand. All it takes is the right recipe and good directions.

The process is even simpler if you use cake mixes. In five minutes you can have a decadent chocolate cake in the oven or a plate of cake-batter rice crispy treats ready to serve. If you want to bake something amazing without spending all day slaving away in the kitchen, this is the cookbook for you.

So play around with the recipes in this book! Mix and match the cakes and buttercreams to create something of your very own! That's the best part of baking! Have fun, eat up, and always remember the story behind every recipe.

Happy baking!
Lizzy

Cupcakes

 Tying your own shoes, taking off the training wheels, and leaving the floaties at home are all standard on the list of growing up. But in my family, learning how to make the perfect s'more is also on the list.

 I remember a trip to Lake Powell for a family reunion when I was about seven. My grandfather scoffed at my cousins, who were sticking their marshmallows deep in the flames and pulling out sizzling, black mallows. They would blow out the flames then pop the mallows in their mouths. My grandfather did not approve. He took great pride in a slow-roasted, perfectly golden, gooey-all-the-way-through marshmallow. I remember him sitting there, teaching me to keep my stick away from the flames and helping me make sure to hover it over the glowing hot coals off to the side—slowly rotating, patiently waiting until the marshmallow was about to fall off the stick—then you knew it was perfect.

BLACK FOREST CUPCAKES

Chocolate Buttermilk Cake:
1 box devil's food cake mix
3 eggs
½ C. oil
¾ C. buttermilk
½ C. sour cream
2 tsp. vanilla extract
1 tsp. almond extract

Whipped Cream Topping:
2 C. heavy whipping cream
1 3.4- to 3.9-oz. pkg. instant white chocolate mousse pudding mix (optional; used to stabilize cream)

Cherry Filling:
1 C. heavy whipping cream
1 C. cherries, pitted and roughly chopped

Chocolate Ganache:
⅓ C. heavy whipping cream
1 C. chocolate chips

Chocolate flakes for decoration
Cherries with stems for decoration

1. Preheat oven to 350 degrees and line pans with cupcake liners.
2. Sift cake mix into a small bowl; set aside.
3. In a large bowl, combine eggs, oil, buttermilk, sour cream, vanilla extract, and almond extract until smooth.
4. Stir in cake mix.
5. Fill cupcake liners ¾ full and bake for 17–22 minutes or until a knife inserted in the center comes out clean.
6. Let cool completely.
7. Whipped Cream Topping: In a stand mixer using a whisk attachment, whip the heavy whipping cream for both the filling and the topping. Add the pudding mix (you can also use unflavored gelatin to help stabilize whipped cream) and whip until stiff peaks form.
8. Cherry Filling: In a medium bowl, gently fold cherries into 1½ C. of the whipped cream.
9. To assemble, use a small knife to cut a "cone" out of the top of each cupcake. Cut off the pointy part of each cone and discard the points. Fill each hole with cherry filling and put the remaining "cap" from the cone over the filling.
10. Chocolate Ganache: Place heavy whipping cream and chocolate chips in a microwave-safe bowl and heat until melted, about 40 seconds. Remove and stir until smooth. Continue to heat in 10-second increments if needed.
11. Spoon chocolate ganache over each filled cupcake and let set for 8–10 minutes.
12. Pipe the remaining whipped cream over the ganache and decorate with chocolate flakes and cherries.

BLACKBERRY LEMONADE CUPCAKES

Lemonade Cake:
1 box white cake mix
3 eggs
⅓ C. oil
Zest of 2 lemons
¼ C. lemon juice
1 tsp. vanilla extract
¾ C. milk
½ C. sour cream

Lemon Glaze:
Zest of half of a lemon
¼ C. lemon juice
1⅔ C. powdered sugar

Blackberry Buttercream:
1 C. butter, softened
4–5 C. powdered sugar
¼ C. pureed blackberries (put blackberries in the blender, blend, then run through a strainer to remove seeds)

Fresh blackberries for decoration

1. Preheat oven to 350 degrees and line pans with cupcake liners.
2. Sift cake mix into a small bowl; set aside.
3. In a large bowl, combine eggs, oil, zest, lemon juice, vanilla extract, milk, and sour cream until smooth.
4. Stir in cake mix.
5. Fill cupcake liners ¾ full and bake for 17–22 minutes or until a knife inserted in the center comes out clean.
6. Lemon Glaze: In a medium bowl, use a whisk or fork to combine all ingredients.
7. Blackberry Buttercream: Beat butter until smooth. Add enough powdered sugar to make the frosting stiff then slowly add pureed blackberries 1 tablespoon at a time until buttercream reaches the desired consistency.
8. Spoon glaze over cooled cupcakes and let set.
9. When glaze is firm, pipe buttercream on top and finish with a fresh blackberry.

S'MORES CUPCAKES

Chocolate Cake:
1 box devil's food cake mix
3 eggs
½ C. melted butter, cooled
½ C. sour cream
1 C. buttermilk or milk
2 tsp. vanilla extract
1½ C. mini chocolate chips

Graham Cracker Frosting:
1 C. butter, softened
2 tsp. vanilla extract
½ tsp. cinnamon
1–3 T. milk, as needed
½ C. graham crackers, finely crushed
3–5 C. powdered sugar

Large marshmallows for decoration
Melted chocolate for decoration

1. Preheat oven to 350 degrees and line pans with cupcake liners.
2. Sift cake mix into a small bowl; set aside.
3. In a large bowl, combine eggs, melted butter, sour cream, buttermilk, and vanilla extract until smooth.
4. Stir in cake mix and chocolate chips.
5. Fill cupcake liners ¾ full and bake for 17–22 minutes or until a knife inserted in the center comes out clean.
6. Graham Cracker Frosting: Beat butter for 2 minutes. Add vanilla extract, cinnamon, 1 T. milk, and graham cracker crumbs (Note: I crush and then put my graham cracker crumbs through a strainer to make sure they are crushed enough and none is too large. It helps to give the frosting a smooth texture.) Add powdered sugar until the frosting reaches the desired consistency; add more milk if needed.
7. Line a cookie sheet with tin foil and place large marshmallows on the foil. Broil in the oven but watch them carefully! They should be slightly brown, which takes only 2–3 minutes; watch them like a hawk or they will burn. Let cool before using.
8. Pipe frosting onto cooled cupcakes. Top with melted chocolate and toasted marshmallows.

DOUBLE CHOCOLATE CUPCAKES FILLED WITH SWEET MASCARPONE

Chocolate Cake:

1 box Devil's food cake mix
3 eggs
½ C. oil
¾ C. buttermilk or milk
½ C. sour cream or plain yogurt
1 tsp. vanilla extract

Mascarpone Filling:

8 oz. mascarpone cheese
⅓ C. powdered sugar
½ tsp. vanilla extract
1 T. hazelnut creamer powder (optional)

Chocolate Malt Buttercream:

½ C. butter, softened
8 oz. cream cheese, softened
2 T. malted milk powder, regular or chocolate
½ C. unsweetened cocoa powder
1 tsp. vanilla extract
2 T. milk
3–4 C. powdered sugar

Chocolate shavings for decoration

1. Preheat oven to 350 degrees and line pans with cupcake liners.
2. Sift cake mix into a small bowl; set aside.
3. In a large bowl, combine eggs, oil, buttermilk, sour cream, and vanilla extract until smooth.
4. Stir in cake mix.
5. Fill liners ¾ full and bake for 17–22 minutes or until a knife inserted in the center comes out clean.
6. Mascarpone Filling: Combine all ingredients in a small bowl using a spoon. Taste and add more sugar if you want it sweeter.
7. Chocolate Malt Buttercream: Beat butter and cream cheese until smooth. Add malted milk powder and cocoa and beat again. Add vanilla and milk; slowly add powdered sugar until buttercream reaches desired consistency. If it becomes too thick, add more milk.
8. To assemble: Use a knife to cut a cone out of the top of each cooled cupcake. Discard cone, fill cavity with a spoonful of filling, and pipe buttercream over filling. Immediately top with chocolate shavings.

PINEAPPLE CREAM CUPCAKES

Pineapple Cake:
1 box yellow cake mix
⅓ C. melted butter, cooled
3 eggs
1¼ C. crushed pineapple with juice
2 tsp. vanilla extract

Cream Cheese Frosting:
½ C. butter, softened
8 oz. cream cheese, softened
1 tsp. vanilla extract
3–4 C. powdered sugar

Maraschino cherries with stems for decoration
Sprinkles for decoration

1. Preheat oven to 350 degrees and line pans with cupcake liners.
2. Sift cake mix into a small bowl; set aside.
3. In a large bowl, combine melted butter, eggs, pineapple, and vanilla extract.
4. Stir in cake mix until smooth.
5. Fill cupcake liners ¾ full and bake for 17–22 minutes or until a knife inserted in the center comes out clean.
6. Let cool.
7. Cream Cheese Frosting: Beat butter and cream cheese for 2 minutes until smooth. Add vanilla extract and slowly add powdered sugar until the frosting reaches the desired consistency. If it becomes too thick, add milk or cream.
8. Pipe frosting onto cooled cupcakes; top with a cherry and sprinkles to dress them up.
9. Bust out a lawn chair and pretend you're on spring break!

CHOCOLATE BANANA CREAM PIE CUPCAKES

Chocolate Banana Cake:

1 box Devil's food cake mix

3 eggs

½ C. oil

3 bananas, mashed

½ C. milk or buttermilk

¼ C. sour cream or plain yogurt (optional)

2 tsp. vanilla extract

Chocolate Buttercream:

1 C. butter, softened

½ C. unsweetened cocoa powder

2 tsp. vanilla extract

3 T. milk

3–4 C. powdered sugar

Banana Cream Filling:

1 3.4- to 3.9-oz. pkg. banana cream instant pudding mix

2 C. heavy whipping cream

1. Preheat oven to 350 degrees and line pans with cupcake liners.
2. Sift cake mix into a small bowl; set aside.
3. In a large bowl, combine eggs, oil, bananas, milk, sour cream, and vanilla extract until smooth.
4. Stir in cake mix until smooth.
5. Fill cupcake liners ¾ full and bake for 17–22 minutes or until a knife inserted in the center comes out clean.
6. Chocolate Buttercream: Beat butter until smooth. Add cocoa, vanilla extract, and milk; beat again. Slowly add powdered sugar until the buttercream reaches the desired consistency.
7. Banana Cream Filling: Using a whisk attachment on a food processor or using a hand mixer, whip cream and pudding mix until stiff peaks form.
8. To Assemble: Pipe a ring of chocolate buttercream around the edge of the cooled cupcakes. Then use a food scoop or a spoon to place the filling in the middle.
9. These are amazing, so go give them away before you take a single bite—or else you'll eat them ALL.

DIRT CUPCAKES

Chocolate Cake:
1 box devil's food or chocolate cake mix
1 3.4- to 3.9-oz. pkg. chocolate pudding mix
4 eggs
⅓ C. oil
1 C. buttermilk or milk
¼ C. sour cream
2 tsp. vanilla extract
13 chocolate sandwich cookies (1 sleeve), roughly chopped

Chocolate Buttercream:
1 C. butter, softened
¾ C. unsweetened cocoa powder
2 T. milk
2 tsp. vanilla extract
3–4 C. powdered sugar

26 chocolate sandwich cookies, crushed, for decoration
Gummy worms for decoration

1. Preheat oven to 350 degrees and line pan with cupcake liners.
2. Sift cake mix and pudding mix together into a small bowl; set aside.
3. In a large bowl, combine eggs, oil, buttermilk, sour cream, and vanilla extract until smooth.
4. Stir in cake mix mixture.
5. Fold in chopped chocolate sandwich cookies.
6. Fill cupcake liners ¾ full and bake for 16–22 minutes or until a knife inserted in the center comes out clean.
7. Let cool.
8. Chocolate Buttercream: Beat butter for 2 minutes. Add cocoa powder, milk, and vanilla extract. Slowly add powdered sugar until buttercream reaches the desired consistency; add more milk if needed.
9. To Assemble: Place a gummy worm on a cupcake, pipe a ring over it, place another gummy, pipe some more frosting, and so on (see photos). Press crushed chocolate sandwich cookies into the frosting and top with a final worm.

CAKE BATTER CUPCAKES

Yellow Sprinkle Cake:
1 box yellow cake mix
⅓ C. oil
3 eggs
⅔ C. buttermilk
⅔ C. sour cream
1 tsp. vanilla extract
¼ C. multicolored sprinkles

Cake Batter Frosting:
½ C. butter, softened
8 oz. cream cheese, softened
1 T. milk
1 tsp. vanilla extract
¼–⅓ C. yellow cake mix (dry)
3–4 C. powdered sugar

Extra sprinkles for decoration

1. Preheat oven to 350 degrees and line pans with cupcake liners.
2. Sift cake mix into a small bowl; set aside.
3. In a large bowl, combine oil, eggs, buttermilk, sour cream, and vanilla extract.
4. Stir in cake mix until smooth.
5. Gently fold in sprinkles. Depending on the type you use, the dye from the sprinkles may start to bleed into the batter, so don't stir too much.
6. Fill cupcake liners ¾ full and bake for 17–22 minutes or until a knife inserted in the center comes out clean.
7. Cake Batter Frosting: Beat butter and cream cheese until smooth. Add milk and vanilla extract. Add ¼ C. yellow cake mix and beat again. Slowly add powdered sugar until the frosting reaches the desired consistency. Taste, and add more yellow cake mix, if needed, to get a stronger flavor.
8. Pipe onto cooled cupcakes and top with more sprinkles!

PEPPERMINT BARK CUPCAKES

Chocolate Cake:
1 box devil's food cake mix
3 eggs
½ C. oil
¾ C. buttermilk or milk
½ C. sour cream or plain yogurt
2 tsp. vanilla extract

Peppermint White Chocolate Chunk Buttercream:
½ C. butter, softened
8 oz. cream cheese (or an extra ½ C. butter)
1½ tsp. peppermint extract
3–4 C. powdered sugar
1 C. white chocolate melts, finely chopped (you can use a food processor)

1½ C. white chocolate melts
Candy canes, crushed, for decoration

1. Preheat oven to 350 degrees and line pans with cupcake liners.
2. Sift cake mix into a small bowl; set aside.
3. In a large bowl, combine eggs, oil, buttermilk, sour cream, and vanilla extract.
4. Mix in cake mix until smooth.
5. Fill cupcake liners ¾ full and bake for 15–20 minutes, or until a knife inserted in the center comes out clean.
6. Peppermint White Chocolate Chunk Buttercream: Beat butter and cream cheese until smooth. Add peppermint extract. Slowly add powdered sugar until the buttercream reaches the desired consistency. Stir in chopped white chocolate.
7. Pipe buttercream onto cooled cupcakes.
8. In a microwave-safe cup, mug, or small bowl that is deep enough to dip the cupcakes, melt the white chocolate melts (regular chocolate chips won't work) in the microwave.
9. Dip each frosted cupcake into the melted chocolate; turn right side up to set.
10. Immediately sprinkle each dipped cupcake with crushed candy cane. Work quickly, because the white chocolate hardens right away.

Note: If you do not want the chocolate to harden like peppermint bark, add 1 T. cream to the melted white chocolate.

CUPCAKES • 19

DOUBLE CHOCOLATE PEANUT BUTTER CUPCAKES

Chocolate Cake:
1 box devil's food cake mix
3 eggs
1 C. milk or buttermilk
½ C. sour cream
1 tsp. vanilla extract
½ C. melted butter, cooled

Peanut Butter Ganache:
⅓ C. creamy peanut butter
⅔ C. chocolate chips or melts

Peanut Butter Chocolate Frosting:
½ C. butter, softened
½ C. creamy peanut butter
½ C. unsweetened cocoa powder
1½ tsp. vanilla extract
1½ T. milk (more if needed)
3–4 C. powdered sugar

Peanut butter cups, chopped, for decoration

1. Preheat oven to 350 degrees and line pans with cupcake liners.
2. Sift cake mix into a small bowl; set aside.
3. In a large bowl, combine remaining cake ingredients until smooth. (Let the melted butter cool a little so it doesn't cook the eggs.)
4. Stir in cake mix.
5. Fill cupcake liners ¾ full and bake for 17–22 minutes or until a knife inserted in the center comes out clean.
6. Let cool.
7. Peanut Butter Ganache: In a small microwave-proof bowl, combine peanut butter and chocolate. Melt in the microwave for about 45 seconds. You can also melt it on the stovetop, stirring until smooth.
8. Dip the tops of cooled cupcakes into the ganache. Turn cupcakes right side up and let the ganache cool for about 15 minutes.
9. Peanut Butter Chocolate Frosting: Beat butter, peanut butter, and cocoa powder for 2 minutes. Scrape down bowl and add vanilla extract and milk. Slowly add powdered sugar until frosting reaches the desired consistency. If it becomes too thick, add more milk.
10. Pipe frosting over the ganache layer and top with chopped peanut butter cups.

COCONUT LIME CUPCAKES

Coconut Cake:
1 box white cake mix
4 egg whites
1 C. coconut milk
⅓ C. oil
½ C. plain yogurt or sour cream
1 T. coconut extract
1 T. vanilla extract

Lime Mascarpone Filling:
8 oz. mascarpone
Zest of 1 lime
2 T. lime juice
½ C. powdered sugar

Lime Cream Cheese Frosting:
8 oz. cream cheese
½ C. butter, softened
Zest of 2 limes
1 T. lime juice
3–4 C. powdered sugar

Shredded coconut for decoration
Sliced limes for decoration

1. Preheat oven to 350 degrees and line pans with cupcakes liners.
2. Sift cake mix into a small bowl to remove lumps; set aside.
3. In a large bowl, combine egg whites, coconut milk, oil, yogurt, coconut extract, and vanilla extract until smooth.
4. Stir in cake mix.
5. Fill cupcake liners ¾ full and bake for 17–22 minutes or until a knife inserted in the center comes out clean.
6. Lime Mascarpone Filling: In a small bowl, mix all ingredients until smooth.
7. Lime Cream Cheese Frosting: Beat cream cheese, butter, and lime zest for 2 minutes. Add lime juice. Slowly add powdered sugar until frosting reaches the desired consistency. Add more lime juice if it becomes too thick.
8. To Assemble: Using a knife, cut a small hole out of the top of each cooled cupcake. Fill each hole with lime mascarpone filling. Pipe frosting over the hole. Roll the top of each cupcake in a bowl of shredded coconut and top with a slice of lime.

RASPBERRY WHITE CHOCOLATE MOUSSE CUPCAKES

Raspberry Vanilla Cake:
1 box white cake mix
3 eggs
⅓ C. melted butter, cooled
1 C. milk or buttermilk
2 tsp. vanilla extract
1½ C. raspberries, fresh or frozen

White Chocolate Quick Mousse:
2 C. heavy whipping cream, cold
1 3.4- to 3.9-oz. pkg. instant white chocolate pudding mix

White chocolate flakes for decoration
Fresh raspberries for decoration

1. Preheat oven to 350 degrees and line pans with cupcakes liners.
2. Sift cake mix into a small bowl; set aside.
3. In a large bowl, combine eggs, butter, milk, and vanilla extract until smooth.
4. Stir in cake mix.
5. Gently fold in raspberries.
6. Fill cupcake liners ¾ full and bake for 17–22 minutes or until a knife inserted in the center comes out clean.
7. Let cupcakes cool completely.
8. White Chocolate Quick Mousse: In a stand mixer using the whisk attachment, whip whipping cream and pudding mix until stiff peaks form.
9. Pipe mousse onto cooled cupcakes and top with white chocolate flakes and fresh raspberries.

Note: If you don't plan on eating the cupcakes the day you make them, store them in the freezer.

SWEET POTATO PIE CUPCAKES WITH BROWN SUGAR BUTTERCREAM

Graham Cracker Crust:
4 T. melted butter
1 C. graham cracker crumbs
1 tsp. sugar

Sweet Potato Cake:
1 box white cake mix
1½ tsp. cinnamon
¼ tsp. cloves (optional)
½ tsp. ginger (optional)
1 tsp. nutmeg
¾ C. sweet potato, cooked and cooled*
3 eggs
⅓ C. oil
½ C. milk
2 tsp. vanilla extract

Brown Sugar Buttercream:
1 C. butter
½ C. brown sugar, packed
1 tsp. vanilla extract
4–5 C. powdered sugar

Pecans or other nuts for decoration

1. Preheat oven to 350 degrees and line pans with cupcake liners.
2. Graham Cracker Crust: In a small bowl, combine melted butter, graham cracker crumbs, and sugar. Press ½–1 T. of the mixture into the bottom of each cupcake liner.
3. Sweet Potato Cake: Sift cake mix, cinnamon, cloves, ginger, and nutmeg into a large bowl; set aside.
4. In a blender, place cooked sweet potato, eggs, oil, milk, and vanilla extract. Blend until smooth. (The blender helps to purée the potato so it's not lumpy in the cupcakes.)
5. Pour mixture over cake mix and spices and stir until smooth.
6. Pour batter over the graham cracker crusts, filling cupcake liners ¾ full, and bake for 17–22 minutes or until a knife inserted in the center comes out clean.
7. Let cool completely.
8. Brown Sugar Buttercream: Beat butter and brown sugar for 2 minutes. Add vanilla extract and slowly add powdered sugar until buttercream reaches the desired consistency. If it is too thick, add 1 T. milk.
9. Pipe buttercream onto cooled cupcakes and top with pecans for decoration.

*To cook the sweet potato, cover a large sweet potato with vegetable oil, put it in a pan lined with foil, and bake at 400 degrees for 35–45 minutes or until tender. Peel and let cool.

CHOCOLATE ALMOND RASPBERRY CUPCAKES

Chocolate Raspberry Cake:

1 box devil's food cake mix

3 eggs

½ C. oil

1 C. buttermilk or milk

⅓ C. sour cream

1 tsp. vanilla extract

1⅓ C. raspberries, fresh or frozen

Chocolate Almond Ganache:

1 C. chocolate chips or melts

⅓ C. heavy whipping cream

1½ tsp. almond extract

Chocolate Buttercream:

1 C. butter, softened

1½ tsp. vanilla extract

1½ tsp. almond extract (optional)

½ C. unsweetened cocoa powder

1–3 T. milk

2½–4 C. powdered sugar

Fresh raspberries for decoration
Sprinkles for decoration

1. Preheat oven to 350 degrees and line pans with cupcake liners.
2. Sift cake mix into a small bowl; set aside.
3. In a large bowl, combine eggs, oil, buttermilk, sour cream, and vanilla extract until smooth.
4. Stir in cake mix.
5. Gently fold in raspberries.
6. Fill cupcake liners ¾ full and bake for 17–22 minutes or until a knife inserted in the center comes out clean.
7. Chocolate Almond Ganache: In a microwave-proof bowl, combine chocolate chips and heavy whipping cream; melt in microwave. Remove from the microwave while there are still chunks of chocolate; stir just until smooth. If necessary, heat for 10 more seconds. Stir in almond extract.
8. Chocolate Buttercream: Beat butter for 2 minutes. Add vanilla extract, almond extract, and cocoa powder; beat again. Add 1 T. milk and gradually add powdered sugar until the buttercream reaches the desired consistency. Add more milk if it gets too thick.
9. To assemble, dip the tops of cooled cupcakes into the ganache and let the ganache set for about 10 minutes (depending on the heat of the room, it may take more or less time). Pipe frosting over the ganache and top with fresh raspberries and sprinkles.

MARASCHINO CHERRY CUPCAKES

Almond-Cherry Cake:
1 box white cake mix
3 eggs
⅓ C. oil
¾ C. milk or buttermilk
½ C. sour cream or plain yogurt
2 tsp. almond extract
1 C. maraschino cherries, roughly chopped

Almond Buttercream:
1 C. butter, softened
1½ tsp. almond extract
3–4 C. powdered sugar
Milk, if needed

Sprinkles for decoration
20–24 maraschino cherries with stems for decoration

1. Preheat oven to 350 degrees and line pans with cupcake liners.
2. Sift cake mix into a small bowl to remove any lumps; set aside.
3. In a large bowl, combine eggs, oil, milk, sour cream, and almond extract until smooth.
4. Stir in cake mix.
5. Fold in chopped maraschino cherries.
6. Fill cupcake liners ¾ full; bake for 17–22 minutes, or until a knife inserted in the center comes out clean.
7. For Almond Buttercream: Beat butter for 2 minutes. Add almond extract. Gradually add powdered sugar until buttercream is the desired consistency. If it gets too thick, add a little milk.
8. Pipe frosting onto cooled cupcakes; top with sprinkles and maraschino cherries.

BLUEBERRY CINNAMON TOAST CRUNCH CUPCAKES

Blueberry Cinnamon Cake:
1 box white cake mix
2 tsp. cinnamon
3 eggs
⅓ C. melted butter, cooled
1 C. buttermilk
2 tsp. vanilla extract
1½ C. blueberries, fresh or frozen

Cinnamon Toast Crunch™ Buttercream:
½ C. Cinnamon Toast Crunch™ cereal, finely crushed
1 C. butter, softened
2 T. milk
1 tsp. vanilla extract
½ tsp. cinnamon
4–5 C. powdered sugar

Cinnamon sugar for decoration
Pieces of Cinnamon Toast Crunch™ cereal for decoration
Fresh blueberries for decoration

1. Preheat oven to 350 degrees and line pans with cupcake liners.
2. Sift cake mix and cinnamon into a small bowl; set aside.
3. In a large bowl, combine eggs, melted butter, buttermilk, and vanilla extract until smooth.
4. Stir in cake mix/cinnamon mixture.
5. Fold in blueberries.
6. Fill cupcake liners ¾ full and bake for 17–22 minutes or until a knife inserted in the center comes out clean.
7. Cinnamon Toast Crunch™ Buttercream: Crush cereal using a food processor or a bag and rolling pin; sift to remove any large pieces. This ensures a silky texture to the frosting. Set crushed cereal aside. Beat butter for 2 minutes. Stir in crushed cereal, milk, vanilla, and cinnamon; beat again. Gradually add powdered sugar until the buttercream reaches the desired consistency.
8. Pipe buttercream onto cooled cupcakes and top with cinnamon sugar, pieces of cereal, and fresh blueberries.

Cinnamon Toast Crunch™ cereal is used with permission of General Mills Marketing Inc. (GMMI).

STRAWBERRY RED VELVET CUPCAKES

Strawberry Red Velvet Cake:
1 box red velvet cake mix
2 T. flour
3 eggs
½ C. melted butter, cooled
½ C. strawberries, pureed in the blender
¼ C. milk
⅔ C. sour cream or plain yogurt
1 tsp. vanilla extract

Cream Cheese Frosting:
½ C. butter, softened
8 oz. cream cheese
2 tsp. vanilla extract
3–4½ C. powdered sugar

Extra strawberries for decoration

1. Preheat oven to 350 degrees and line pans with cupcake liners.
2. Sift cake mix and flour into a small bowl; set aside.
3. In a large bowl, combine eggs, melted butter, strawberry puree, milk, sour cream, and vanilla extract.
4. Stir in cake mix and flour.
5. Fill cupcake liners ¾ full and bake for 17–22 minutes or until a knife inserted near the center comes out clean.
6. Cream Cheese Frosting: Beat softened butter and cream cheese for 2 minutes. Add vanilla and 3 C. powdered sugar. Beat well. Gradually add more powdered sugar until the frosting reaches the desired consistency.
7. Pipe frosting onto cooled cupcakes; top with fresh strawberries.

Bundt Cakes

Most kids ride bikes up and down their driveways, but my brothers and I preferred to eat our way up and down the driveway instead. Our long, windy driveway was lined with blueberry bushes. Our fingertips were dyed purple every day from the end of June to August, and our lips were still tinged with the color when we woke up each morning. We spent our summer days hiding deep in the bushes from our mother when she called us in to clean our dirty rooms. And if we didn't care for what was on the table for breakfast, we just wandered outside for a handful of warm blueberries.

BLUEBERRY ALMOND MINI BUNDT CAKE

Blueberry Almond Cake:
1 box white cake mix
1 3.4- to 3.9-oz. pkg. instant vanilla or white chocolate pudding mix
4 eggs
⅔ C. oil
½ C. milk or buttermilk
1 C. sour cream
1 tsp. vanilla extract
2 tsp. almond extract
½ tsp. nutmeg (optional)
1½ C. blueberries, fresh or frozen

Orange Glaze:
2 T. orange juice (can also use lemon juice or milk)
1 T. milk
1½–2½ C. powdered sugar

Sliced almonds and fresh blueberries for decoration

1. Preheat oven to 350 degrees and grease mini Bundt pans or one regular Bundt pan.
2. Sift cake mix and instant pudding mix into a small bowl; set aside.
3. In a large bowl, combine eggs, oil, milk, sour cream, vanilla extract, almond extract, and nutmeg until smooth.
4. Stir in cake mix mixture.
5. Fold in blueberries.
6. Fill mini Bundt pans about ⅔ full and bake for 18–25 minutes or until a knife inserted near the center comes out clean. (It's okay if they bake over the center notch; mine did, and they hold the glaze quite nicely!) If you use a single regular-sized Bundt pan, bake for 35–45 minutes or until a knife inserted near the center comes out clean.
7. Let cool in pans, then turn out.
8. Orange Glaze: Combine all ingredients and whisk. Add more powdered sugar if you want a thicker glaze or more milk or juice to thin it out. It should be pourable.
9. Pour glaze over cooled cakes, sprinkle with sliced almonds, and fill the holes with blueberries.

CHOCOLATE ZUCCHINI BUNDT CAKE

Chocolate Zucchini Cake:
1 box Devil's food cake mix
1 3.4- to 3.9-oz. pkg. chocolate instant pudding mix
4 eggs
⅔ C. oil
1 C. sour cream
½ C. buttermilk
1 tsp. vanilla extract
2 C. zucchini, grated
1½ C. mini chocolate chips

Cinnamon Glaze:
3 T. butter, melted
2–4 T. milk
1½ C. powdered sugar
¼ tsp. cinnamon

1. Preheat oven to 350 degrees and grease a Bundt pan well.
2. Sift cake mix into a small bowl to remove any lumps; add pudding mix. Set aside.
3. In a large bowl, combine eggs, oil, sour cream, buttermilk, and vanilla extract until smooth.
4. Add cake mix mixture and stir.
5. Stir in grated zucchini and mini chocolate chips.
6. Dump batter into prepared Bundt pan and spread evenly.
7. Bake for 40–55 minutes or until a knife inserted near the center comes out with no batter on it. (There will be melted chocolate from the chocolate chips, but that's okay.)
8. Let cool in pan and then turn out.
9. Cinnamon Glaze: Whisk butter, 2 T. milk, powdered sugar, and cinnamon until smooth. Add more milk, if needed, to get a pourable consistency.
10. Pour glaze over cake and enjoy!

RASPBERRY WHITE CHOCOLATE BUNDT CAKE

Raspberry Cake:
1 box white cake mix
1 3.4- to 3.9-oz. pkg. instant white chocolate or vanilla pudding mix
1 egg
4 egg whites
⅔ C. oil
¾ C. milk or buttermilk
¾ C. sour cream
1 tsp. vanilla extract
1½ C. white chocolate chips
1½ C. raspberries

Cream Cheese Glaze:
2 T. butter
2–3 T. milk or heavy cream
1 tsp. vanilla extract
1½ C. powdered sugar

Raspberries for decoration
Grated white chocolate for decoration

1. Preheat oven to 350 degrees and grease a Bundt pan well.
2. Sift cake mix and pudding mix into a small bowl; set aside.
3. In a large bowl, combine egg, egg whites, oil, milk, sour cream, and vanilla extract until smooth.
4. Stir in cake mix mixture.
5. Stir in white chocolate chips.
6. Gently fold in raspberries.
7. Dump batter into prepared Bundt pan and spread evenly.
8. Bake for 35–45 minutes or until a knife inserted near the center comes out clean.
9. Let cool completely.
10. Cream Cheese Glaze: Combine butter and 2 T. milk; melt until smooth. Whisk in vanilla extract and 1 C. powdered sugar. Make glaze thicker with more powdered sugar or thinner with more milk.
11. To assemble, flip Bundt pan to release cooled cake, pour warm glaze over cake, and decorate with extra raspberries and grated white chocolate.

BREAKFAST BUNDT CAKE

Cinnamon Blueberry Buttermilk Cake:
1 box white cake mix
4 eggs
⅔ C. melted butter, cooled
¾ C. buttermilk or milk
1 C. sour cream or plain yogurt
2 tsp. vanilla extract
1 T. cinnamon
1 3.4- to 3.9-oz. pkg. vanilla or white chocolate instant pudding mix
1½ C. blueberries

Maple Glaze:
2 C. powdered sugar
2 T. butter, melted
1 tsp. maple flavoring
2–4 T. milk

5 pieces of bacon, cooked and chopped for decoration

1. Preheat oven to 350 degrees and grease a Bundt pan.
2. Sift cake mix into a small bowl to remove any lumps; set aside.
3. In a large bowl, combine eggs, butter, buttermilk, sour cream, and vanilla extract.
4. Add cake mix, cinnamon, and instant pudding mix; stir until combined.
5. Fold in blueberries.
6. Dump batter into prepared Bundt pan and spread evenly.
7. Bake for 38–50 minutes or until a knife inserted near the center comes out clean.
8. Let cool in pan, then turn out.
9. Maple Glaze: Whisk powdered sugar, butter, maple flavoring, and 2 T. milk together until smooth. If too thick to pour, add more milk.
10. Pour glaze over cooled cake and top with chopped bacon.

HOT CHOCOLATE BUNDT CAKE

Chocolate Cake:
1 box devil's food or chocolate cake mix
1 3.4- to 3.9-oz. pkg. instant chocolate pudding mix
2 T. unsweetened cocoa powder
¾ C. oil
4 eggs
¾ C. milk
1 C. sour cream
2 tsp. vanilla extract

Hot Chocolate Glaze:
2 T. dry hot chocolate mix
3 T. butter
2–3 T. milk
1 T. cocoa powder, unsweetened
1½ C. powdered sugar

Mini marshmallows for decoration

1. Preheat oven to 350 degrees and grease a Bundt pan well.
2. Sift cake mix, pudding mix, and cocoa powder into a small bowl; set aside.
3. In a large bowl, combine oil, eggs, milk, sour cream, and vanilla extract until smooth.
4. Stir in cake mix mixture until smooth.
5. Dump batter into prepared Bundt pan and spread evenly.
6. Bake for 35–45 minutes or until a knife inserted near the center comes out clean.
7. Let cool completely.
8. Hot Chocolate Glaze: In a medium-sized microwave-proof bowl, melt hot chocolate mix, butter, and 2 T. milk. Whisk until smooth. Add cocoa powder and 1 C. powdered sugar. To make thicker, add more powdered sugar. To make thinner, add more milk.
9. To assemble, flip Bundt pan to release cooled cake. Pour warm glaze over the cake and top with mini marshmallows.

BANANA BUNDT WITH CHOCOLATE GLAZE AND WALNUTS

Banana Cake:

1 box white cake mix
2 bananas, mashed
2 T. brown sugar
3 eggs
1 C. sour cream
½ C. melted butter, cooled
½ C. buttermilk
1½ tsp. vanilla extract
1½ C. mini chocolate chips, optional

Chocolate Glaze:

1 C. chocolate chips
¾ C. heavy whipping cream

Walnuts for decoration

1. Preheat oven to 350 degrees and grease a Bunt pan well.
2. Sift cake mix into a small bowl to remove any lumps; set aside.
3. In a large bowl, mash bananas using a fork.
4. Add brown sugar, eggs, sour cream, butter, buttermilk, and vanilla extract; stir until combined.
5. Add cake mix and stir well. Add chocolate chips if desired.
6. Dump batter into prepared pan and spread evenly.
7. Bake for 35–45 minutes or until a knife inserted near the center comes out clean.
8. Let cool in pan, then turn out.
9. Chocolate Glaze: In a double-boiler on the stove or in a medium bowl in the microwave, combine chocolate chips and heavy cream; melt. Stir until smooth.
10. Pour glaze over cooled cake and top with walnuts. If you want your glaze to be a little thicker, let it cool a little before you pour it over the cake.

LEMON BLUEBERRY POPPY SEED BUNDT CAKE

Lemon Blueberry Poppy Seed Cake:

1 box white cake mix

4 eggs

⅔ C. oil

Zest of 2 lemons

¼ C. lemon juice

½ C. milk

1 C. plain yogurt

1 3.4- to 3.9-oz. pkg. lemon instant pudding mix

1 T. poppy seeds

1½ C. blueberries, fresh or frozen

Lemon Glaze:

1½ C. powdered sugar

3 T. lemon juice

2 T. butter, melted

Fresh blueberries for decoration

1. Preheat oven to 350 degrees and grease a Bundt pan.
2. Sift cake mix into a small bowl to remove any lumps; set aside.
3. In a large bowl, combine eggs, oil, lemon zest, lemon juice, milk, and yogurt.
4. Add cake mix and instant pudding mix; stir well.
5. Stir in poppy seeds.
6. Gently fold in blueberries.
7. Dump into Bundt pan and spread evenly.
8. Bake for 38–50 minutes or until a knife inserted near the center comes out clean.
9. Let cool in pan and then turn out.
10. Lemon Glaze: Whisk powdered sugar, lemon juice, and butter. Add more lemon juice if you want a thinner glaze or more powdered sugar to make it thicker.
11. Pour glaze over the cooled cake and serve with fresh blueberries.

DARK CHOCOLATE BUNDT CAKE

Dark Chocolate Cake:
1 box devil's food cake mix
4 eggs
¾ C. oil
¾ C. buttermilk or milk
1 C. sour cream or plain yogurt
2 tsp. vanilla extract
1 3.4- to 3.9-oz. pkg. instant chocolate pudding mix
1½ C. dark chocolate chips, chopped in a blender

Chocolate Glaze:
¾ C. dark chocolate chips
3 T. butter, melted
1 T. light corn syrup

Raspberries for decoration and color

1. Preheat oven to 350 degrees and grease a Bundt pan well.
2. Sift cake mix into a small bowl; set aside.
3. In a large bowl, combine eggs, oil, buttermilk, sour cream, and vanilla extract.
4. Stir in cake mix and pudding mix.
5. Add chocolate chips and stir again.
6. Dump batter into Bundt pan and spread evenly.
7. Bake for 38–50 minutes or until a knife inserted near the center comes out clean.
8. Let cool in pan, then turn out.
9. Chocolate Glaze: Combine all ingredients and whisk until smooth.
10. Pour glaze over cooled cake and fill the center with raspberries.

MINI CHERRY ALMOND BUNDTS

Cherry Almond Cake:
1 box white cake mix
4 eggs
⅔ C. oil
¾ C. milk
1 C. sour cream
2 tsp. almond extract
1 3.4- to 3.9-oz. pkg. instant white chocolate or vanilla pudding mix
1 C. maraschino cherries, roughly chopped

Cherry Glaze:
1½ C. powdered sugar
3 T. maraschino cherry syrup (the juice in which the cherries are bottled)
2 T. butter, melted

Maraschino cherries with stems for decoration

1. Preheat oven to 350 degrees and grease mini or regular-sized Bundt pan(s) well.
2. Sift cake mix into a small bowl; set aside.
3. In a large bowl, combine eggs, oil, milk, sour cream, and almond extract until smooth.
4. Stir in cake mix and pudding mix.
5. Fold in maraschino cherries.
6. Fill mini Bundt pans ¾ full and bake for 18–25 minutes; pour batter into a regular-sized Bundt pan, spread batter evenly, and bake 35–45 minutes, or until a knife inserted near the center comes out clean.
7. Let cake cool completely before turning out.
8. Cherry Glaze: Whisk powdered sugar, maraschino cherry syrup, and melted butter until smooth. Add more powdered sugar if you want the glaze to be thicker, or add more cherry syrup to thin it out.
9. Pour glaze over cooled cakes and top with maraschino cherries.

BUNDT CAKES • 55

PEACHES AND CREAM BUNDT CAKE

Peach Cake:
1 box white cake mix
1 3.4- to 3.9-oz. pkg. instant vanilla or white chocolate pudding mix
½ C. pureed peaches (to make puree, place skinned, sliced peaches in a blender)
¼ C. milk
1 C. sour cream or plain yogurt
¾ C. melted butter, cooled
4 eggs
2–3 fresh peaches, sliced

Cream Cheese Glaze:
3 oz. cream cheese
1 T. butter
1 C. powdered sugar
2–4 T. milk

Fresh peaches for garnish

1. Preheat oven to 350 degrees and grease a Bundt pan well.
2. Sift cake mix into a small bowl to remove any lumps; add pudding mix and set aside.
3. In a large bowl, combine pureed peaches, milk, sour cream, melted butter, and eggs.
4. Stir in cake mix mixture until smooth.
5. Dump batter into prepared pan and spread evenly.
6. Place peach slices on top of the batter, fanning them around in a circle; gently press into the cake.
7. Bake for 40–50 minutes or until a knife inserted near the center comes out clean.
8. Let cool in pan, then turn out.
9. Cream Cheese Glaze: In a microwave-safe bowl, place cream cheese and butter; heat for 20 seconds. Add powdered sugar and 2 T. milk and whisk until smooth. Add more milk if the glaze is too thick.
10. Pour glaze over cooled cake and serve with fresh peaches.

PUMPKIN BUNDT CAKE

Pumpkin Cake:
1 box spice cake mix
3 eggs
½ C. oil or applesauce
¼ C. milk
¼ C. sour cream or plain yogurt
15 oz. pureed pumpkin
2 tsp. vanilla extract

Cream Cheese Frosting:
4 oz. cream cheese
3 T. butter, softened
1½ C. powdered sugar
1 tsp. vanilla extract

Nuts and/or chocolate chips for decoration

1. Preheat oven to 350 degrees and grease a Bundt pan well.
2. Sift cake mix into a small bowl to remove any lumps; set aside.
3. In a large bowl, combine eggs, oil, milk, sour cream, pureed pumpkin, and vanilla extract until smooth.
4. Stir in cake mix.
5. Dump batter into prepared pan and spread evenly.
6. Bake for 40–50 minutes or until a knife inserted near the center comes out clean.
7. Let cool in pan, then turn out.
8. Cream Cheese Frosting: Beat cream cheese, butter, powdered sugar, and vanilla extract until smooth.
9. Pipe frosting over cooled cake or add a few tablespoons of milk if you want to create a glaze you can pour over the cake. Top with nuts or chocolate chips for decoration.

PINEAPPLE CAKE WITH SWEET STRAWBERRIES

Pineapple Upside-Down Cake:

1 box yellow cake mix

3 eggs

½ C. melted butter, cooled

⅓ C. pineapple juice

½ C. milk or buttermilk

⅔ C. sour cream or plain yogurt

1 tsp. vanilla extract

3 T. melted butter

¼ C. brown sugar

7 pineapple rings

Sweet Strawberries:

3 C. strawberries, sliced

3 T. sugar

Fresh strawberries for decoration

1. Preheat oven to 350 degrees and grease a Bundt pan well.
2. Sift cake mix into a small bowl to remove any lumps; set aside.
3. In a large bowl, combine eggs, ½ C. melted butter, pineapple juice, milk, sour cream, and vanilla extract until smooth.
4. Add cake mix and stir well.
5. In another small bowl, combine 3 T. melted butter with brown sugar; stir until smooth.
6. Pour brown sugar-butter mixture into the bottom of the prepared Bundt pan.
7. Place pineapple rings over the brown sugar mixture and arrange them to be as flat as possible in the pan.
8. Pour cake batter over pineapple rings and spread evenly.
9. Bake for 40–50 minutes or until a knife inserted near the center comes out clean.
10. Let cool in pan, then turn out.
11. Sweet Strawberries: Gently fold sliced strawberries and sugar together. Let sit for a few minutes while the sugar pulls out the juices from the berries. Pour over cake.
12. Fill the hole of the Bundt with extra berries for decoration.

BIRTHDAY BUNDT CAKE

Yellow Cake:
1 box yellow cake mix
3 eggs
½ C. oil
¾ C. milk
¾ C. plain yogurt or sour cream

Glaze:
3 T. butter, melted
2–4 T. milk
1¾ C. powdered sugar

Sprinkles for decoration

1. Preheat oven to 350 degrees and grease a Bundt pan well.
2. Sift the cake mix into a small bowl to remove any lumps; set aside.
3. In a large bowl, combine eggs, oil, milk, and yogurt until smooth.
4. Stir in cake mix.
5. Dump batter into prepared pan and spread evenly.
6. Bake for 40–50 minutes or until a knife inserted near the center comes out clean.
7. Let cool in pan, then turn out.
8. Glaze: Whisk butter, 2 T. milk, and powdered sugar until smooth. Add more milk, if needed, to get a pourable consistency; if you want to pipe on the glaze, keep it at a thicker consistency.
9. Glaze cake and cover with sprinkles.

CHOCOLATE STRAWBERRY BUNDT CAKE

Chocolate Cake with Strawberry Swirl:
1 box devil's food cake mix
4 eggs
⅔ C. oil
¾ C. buttermilk or milk
⅔ C. sour cream
1 tsp. vanilla extract
½ C. strawberry jam

Chocolate Glaze:
3 T. butter, melted
¼ C. unsweetened cocoa powder
1¼ C. powdered sugar
2–4 T. milk

Fresh strawberries for decoration

1. Preheat oven to 350 degrees and grease a Bundt pan well.
2. Sift cake mix into a small bowl to remove any lumps; set aside.
3. In a large bowl, combine eggs, oil, buttermilk, sour cream, and vanilla extract until smooth.
4. Stir in cake mix.
5. Dump half the batter in the prepared pan and spread evenly.
6. Pour strawberry jam over the batter and spread evenly.
7. Pour the remaining batter on top of the jam layer and spread evenly.
8. Bake for 35–45 minutes or until a knife inserted near the center comes out clean.
9. Let cool in pan and then turn out.
10. Chocolate Glaze: Whisk butter, cocoa powder, powdered sugar, and 2 T. milk until smooth. Add more milk, if needed, until glaze is a pourable consistency.
11. Pour glaze over cooled cake and decorate with strawberries.

RASPBERRY LEMONADE BUNDT CAKE

Lemon Cake:
1 box white cake mix
1 3.4- to 3.9-oz. pkg. instant lemon pudding mix
4 eggs
⅔ C. oil
⅔ C. milk
Zest of 1 lemon
¼ C. lemon juice
⅔ C. plain yogurt

Raspberry Swirl:
1 C. raspberries
3 T. sugar
2 T. cake batter

Lemon Glaze:
2 T. melted butter
2 T. lemon juice
1⅓ C. powdered sugar

Fresh raspberries for decoration

1. Preheat oven to 350 degrees and grease a Bundt pan well.
2. Sift cake mix into a small bowl to remove any lumps; add pudding mix.
3. In a large bowl, combine eggs, oil, milk, lemon zest, lemon juice, and plain yogurt.
4. Add cake mix mixture and stir well.
5. Raspberry Swirl: In a blender, puree raspberries and sugar. Press through a sieve to remove seeds. Mix 2 T. of cake batter into the seedless raspberry-sugar mixture.
6. Pour ½ of the cake batter into the prepared pan and spread evenly.
7. Pour raspberry swirl over cake batter and spread evenly.
8. Dump remaining batter over the raspberry layer and spread evenly.
9. Bake for 40–55 minutes or until a knife inserted near the center comes out clean.
10. Let cool in pan, then turn out.
11. Lemon Glaze: Whisk melted butter, lemon juice, and powdered sugar until smooth. Add more powdered sugar to make the glaze thicker or more lemon juice to make it thinner.
12. Pour glaze over cooled cake and serve with fresh raspberries.

CINNAMON SWIRL BUNDT CAKE

Vanilla Cake:
1 box white cake mix
4 eggs
⅔ C. butter, melted
1 C. sour cream
2 tsp. vanilla extract
1 3.4- to 3.9-oz. pkg. vanilla or white chocolate instant pudding mix

Cinnamon Swirl:
⅓ C. brown sugar
1½ T. ground cinnamon

Cream Cheese Glaze:
3 oz. cream cheese
2 T. butter
¾ C. powdered sugar
2–4 T. milk

1. Preheat oven to 350 degrees and grease a Bundt pan well.
2. Sift cake mix into a small bowl to remove any lumps; set aside.
3. In a large bowl, combine eggs, butter, sour cream, and vanilla extract until smooth.
4. Stir in cake mix and pudding mix.
5. Cinnamon Swirl: In a small bowl, combine brown sugar and cinnamon.
6. Dump roughly ⅓ of the vanilla cake batter into the prepared pan and spread evenly.
7. Sprinkle ½ of the Cinnamon Swirl mixture over the batter.*
8. Dump another ⅓ of the batter over the cinnamon layer and spread evenly.
9. Sprinkle the remaining cinnamon mixture over the batter. Cover with the last of the cake batter, spreading it evenly.
10. Bake for 40–50 minutes or until a knife inserted near the center comes out clean.
11. Let cool completely, then turn out.
12. Cream Cheese Glaze: In a microwave-safe bowl, combine cream cheese and butter; heat for 20 seconds. Add powdered sugar and 2 T. milk and whisk until smooth. Add more milk, if needed, to thin the glaze.
13. Pour glaze over cooled cake.

*Note: Avoid getting the Cinnamon Swirl mixture directly on the pan, because it will stick when you turn out the cooled cake.

ORANGE CRANBERRY BUNDT CAKE

Orange Cranberry Cake:
1 box white cake mix
1 3.4- to 3.9-oz. pkg. instant vanilla pudding
4 eggs
⅔ C. oil
⅔ C. orange juice
Zest of 2 oranges
1 C. sour cream
2 tsp. vanilla extract
1½ C. fresh or dried cranberries

Orange Glaze:
2 T. unsalted butter
2 C. powdered sugar, sifted
2 oranges, juiced and zested

1. Preheat oven to 350 degrees and generously spray a Bundt pan with nonstick cooking spray.
2. Sift cake mix and pudding mix together; set aside.
3. In a large bowl, combine eggs, oil, orange juice, orange zest, sour cream, and vanilla extract.
4. Stir in sifted cake mix and cranberries.
5. Dump the batter into the Bundt pan and spread it out evenly.
6. Bake for 40–50 minutes or until a knife inserted near the center comes out clean.
7. Let cool and then turn the cake out of the pan.
8. Orange Glaze: Combine all glaze ingredients and whisk until smooth. If the glaze is too thin, add more powdered sugar to thicken.

Layered Cakes

Growing up with two older brothers can sometimes mean war. The ammo of choice? Andes mint wrappers. Twist one around your fingertip to make a long pointy "dagger" at one end, and place the open end in your mouth. Then just puff air in your enemy's direction. Immature? Sure. But I was six and merely defending myself!

ANDES MINT CAKE

Chocolate Cake:

1 box devil's food cake mix
3 eggs
½ C. oil
¾ C. buttermilk or milk
¾ C. sour cream
2 tsp. vanilla extract

Green Minty Cream Filling:

1¼ C. butter, softened
1½ tsp. peppermint extract
2 T. milk
4–5 C. powdered sugar
Green food dye (optional)

Chocolate Mint Buttercream:

1¼ C. butter, softened
½ C. unsweetened cocoa powder
1½ tsp. peppermint extract
2 T. milk or sour cream
3–4 C. powdered sugar

Chocolate Ganache:

¾ C. chocolate chips
½ C. heavy whipping cream

Andes mints for decoration

1. Preheat oven to 350 degrees and grease three 8-inch pans. (You can also use only two pans; see baking time below.) I prefer to line the bottoms of my pans with foil or parchment paper for easy removal.
2. Sift cake mix into a small bowl; set aside.
3. In a large bowl, whisk eggs, oil, buttermilk, sour cream, and vanilla extract until smooth.
4. Stir in cake mix.
5. Pour equal amount of batter into each prepared pan and use a spatula to spread evenly. Bake for 17–22 minutes or until a knife inserted near the center comes out clean. (If you are making only two layers, the cake will need to bake for 20–25 minutes.)
6. Let cake cool completely.
7. Green Minty Cream Filling: Beat butter for 2 minutes. Add peppermint extract and milk and beat again. Gradually add powdered sugar until the filling reaches the desired consistency.
8. Chocolate Mint Buttercream: Beat butter for 2 minutes. Add cocoa powder, peppermint extract, and milk; beat again. Gradually add powdered sugar until the buttercream reaches the desired consistency.
9. Chocolate Ganache: In a microwave-safe bowl, combine chocolate chips and heavy whipping cream. Microwave for 30 seconds. Stir. Continue to microwave in 10-second increments until smooth.
10. To assemble the cake, place one layer of chocolate cake on a cake stand; frost with the Green Minty Cream Filling. Top with a second layer of cake; frost with the rest of the filling. Top with the last layer of cake; frost the top and sides with Chocolate Mint Buttercream.
11. Use Andes mint candies to decorate the bottom of the cake.
12. Pour the Chocolate Ganache carefully over the top of the cake and let it drip down the sides. Finish with chopped Andes mints on top.

BIRTHDAY CAKE

Confetti Cake:
1 box white or yellow cake mix
1 3.4- to 3.9-oz. pkg. instant vanilla pudding mix
4 eggs
¾ C. melted butter, cooled
1 C. milk
1 C. sour cream
2 tsp. vanilla extract
½ tsp. almond extract, optional
⅓ C. multicolored sprinkles

Cake Batter Buttercream:
2½ C. butter
½ C. yellow cake mix, sifted
2 tsp. vanilla extract
2 T. milk
5–6 C. powdered sugar

Sprinkles for decoration
Maraschino cherries with stems for decoration

1. Preheat oven to 350 degrees and grease three 8-inch pans. (You can make this cake with only two layers; see baking time below.) I like to line the bottoms with foil or parchment paper for easy cleanup and removal.
2. Sift cake mix and pudding mix into a small bowl; set aside.
3. In a large bowl, combine eggs, butter, milk, sour cream, vanilla extract, and almond extract.
4. Stir in cake mix.
5. Gently fold in sprinkles. (The sprinkles tend to bleed their colors into the batter, so don't stir too much.)
6. Divide batter between prepared pans and use a spatula to spread out evenly. Bake for 17–22 minutes or until a knife inserted near the center comes out clean.
7. Let cake cool completely.
8. Cake Batter Buttercream: Beat butter and cake mix for 2 minutes. Add vanilla extract and milk; gradually add powdered sugar until the buttercream reaches the desired consistency.
9. To assemble the cake, stack the layers, spreading buttercream between each layer; after the layers are stacked, cover the entire cake with remaining buttercream. "Pat" handfuls of sprinkles on the side of the cake. Pipe extra frosting in little swirls on top and decorate with cherries.

CHOCOLATE HAZELNUT CAKE

Chocolate Cake:
1 box devil's food cake mix
1 3.4- to 3.9-oz. pkg. instant pudding mix
4 eggs
¾ C. oil
¾ C. buttermilk
1 C. sour cream
2 tsp. vanilla extract

Chocolate Hazelnut Buttercream:
1½ C. butter, softened
1 C. chocolate hazelnut spread
¼ C. unsweetened cocoa powder
2 tsp. vanilla extract
3 T. milk or sour cream
5–6 C. powdered sugar

Hazelnuts for decoration

1. Preheat oven to 350 degrees and grease three 8-inch pans. (You can make this cake with only two layers; see baking time below.) I like to line the bottoms of my pans with foil or parchment for easy removal.
2. Sift cake mix and instant pudding mix into a small bowl; set aside.
3. In a large bowl, combine eggs, oil, buttermilk, sour cream, and vanilla extract; whisk until smooth.
4. Stir in cake and pudding mix.
5. Divide evenly between prepared pans and use a spatula to spread the batter evenly. Bake for 17–22 minutes or until a knife inserted near the center comes out clean. (If you are making only two layers, bake for 20–25 minutes.)
6. Let cake cool completely.
7. Chocolate Hazelnut Buttercream: In a large bowl, combine butter and chocolate hazelnut spread; beat for 2 minutes. Add cocoa powder and vanilla extract; beat again. Stir in milk; gradually add powdered sugar until the buttercream reaches the desired consistency.
8. To assemble the cake, stack the layers, spreading buttercream between each layer; after all layers are stacked, cover the entire cake with remaining buttercream. Decorate with crushed hazelnuts.

COOKIE DOUGH CAKE

Chocolate Chip Cake:
1 box white cake mix
3 eggs
½ C. melted butter, cooled
¾ C. buttermilk or milk
¾ C. sour cream
⅓ C. brown sugar
1 T. vanilla extract
1 C. mini chocolate chips

Cookie Dough Frosting:
2 C. butter, softened
⅔ C. brown sugar
3 tsp. vanilla extract
⅔ C. flour
1 tsp. salt
5–6 C. powdered sugar
⅔ C. mini chocolate chips, for filling

Decoration:
1½ C. mini chocolate chips
8 chocolate chip cookies
⅓ C. crushed chocolate chip cookies

1. Preheat oven to 350 degrees and grease three 8-inch pans. (You can make this cake with only two layers; see baking time below.) I like to line the bottoms of my pans with foil or parchment for easy removal.
2. Sift cake mix into a small bowl; set aside.
3. In a large bowl, use a whisk to combine eggs, melted butter, buttermilk, sour cream, brown sugar, and vanilla extract until smooth.
4. Stir in cake mix and 1 C. mini chocolate chips.
5. Divide batter evenly between prepared pans and use a spatula to spread the batter evenly. Bake for 17–22 minutes or until a knife inserted near the center comes out clean. (If you are making only two layers, bake for 20–25 minutes.)
6. Let cake cool completely.
7. Cookie Dough Frosting: In a large bowl, beat butter and brown sugar for 2 minutes. Add vanilla extract, flour, and salt; beat again. Gradually add powdered sugar until frosting reaches the desired consistency.
8. Remove about 2 C. of frosting to use between cake layers; stir the ⅔ C. mini chocolate chips into the 2 C. frosting.
9. To assemble the cake, stack layers, frosting between each with the frosting/chocolate chip mixture. Top with the final layer of cake and cover the cake with the rest of the frosting. (Save a little frosting to pipe decorations on top of the finished cake, if desired.)
10. Use mini chocolate chips to cover the sides of the cake; decorate the top with piped frosting, cookies, and crushed cookies.

80 • LAYERED CAKES

HAWAIIAN VACATION CAKE

Haupia (Creamy Coconut Filling):
1 can coconut milk
1 C. sugar
1 C. milk
½ C. water
½ C. cornstarch

Pineapple Mango Cake:
1 box yellow or white cake mix
3 eggs
½ C. oil
1 mango, peeled, pitted, and pureed in a blender
1 C. crushed pineapple
1 tsp. vanilla extract
¼ C. sour cream or plain yogurt

Coconut Buttercream:
1¼ C. butter, softened
8 oz. cream cheese
3 tsp. coconut extract
2 T. milk
4–6 C. powdered sugar

Flaked coconut for decoration
Wedges of fresh pineapple for decoration

1. Haupia: In a saucepan over medium-high heat, bring coconut milk, sugar, and milk to a boil; reduce heat to simmer. In a small bowl, combine water and cornstarch. Whisk water-cornstarch mixture into hot coconut mixture and heat until thick, stirring, about 5 minutes. Let cool completely and refrigerate until ready to use.
2. Preheat oven to 350 degrees and grease three 8-inch pans. (You can make this cake with only two layers; see baking time below.) I like to use foil or parchment paper to line the bottoms of my pans for easy cleanup and removal.
3. Sift cake mix into a small bowl; set aside.
4. In a large bowl, combine eggs, oil, mango, pineapple, vanilla extract, and sour cream.
5. Stir in cake mix.
6. Divide batter between prepared pans and use a spatula to spread out evenly. Bake for 17–22 minutes or until a knife inserted near the center comes out clean. (If you are making only two layers, bake for 20–25 minutes.)
7. Let cake cool completely.
8. Coconut Buttercream: In a large bowl, beat butter and cream cheese for 2 minutes. Stir in coconut extract and milk; gradually add powdered sugar until buttercream reaches the desired consistency.
9. To assemble the cake, stack the layers, spreading the Haupia filling between each layer. Pipe a "dam" of Coconut Buttercream around the edge of the bottom two cake layers to keep the Haupia from gushing out the sides of the cake. Once layers are stacked, cover the cake with Coconut Buttercream and flaked coconut. Top with pieces of fresh pineapple.

CHOCOLATE MALT CAKE

Chocolate Malt Cake:
1 box devil's food cake mix
½ C. malted milk powder, regular or chocolate
3 eggs
½ C. melted butter, cooled
½ C. buttermilk or milk
1 C. sour cream
2 tsp. vanilla extract

Chocolate Malt Buttercream:
2 C. butter, softened
8 oz. cream cheese
¾ C. unsweetened cocoa powder
⅓ C. malted milk powder, regular or chocolate
2 tsp. vanilla extract
¼ C. milk or sour cream
5–6 C. powdered sugar

Extra malted milk balls for decoration

1. Preheat oven to 350 degrees and grease three 8-inch pans. (You can make this cake with only two layers; see baking time below.) I like to use foil or parchment paper to line the bottom of my pans for easy cleanup and removal.
2. Sift cake mix and ½ C. malted milk powder into a small bowl; set aside.
3. In a large bowl, combine eggs, butter, buttermilk, sour cream, and vanilla extract.
4. Stir in cake mix and malted milk powder.
5. Divide into prepared pans and use a spatula to smooth out evenly.
6. Bake for 17–22 minutes or until a knife inserted near the center comes out clean. (If you are making only two layers, bake for 20–25 minutes.)
7. Let cake cool completely.
8. Chocolate Malt Buttercream: In a large bowl, beat butter and cream cheese for 2 minutes. Add cocoa and ⅓ C. malted milk powder; beat again. Stir in vanilla extract and milk; gradually add powdered sugar 1 C. at a time until buttercream reaches the desired consistency. If it becomes too thick, add more milk.
9. To assemble the cake, stack the layers, using an offset spatula to spread buttercream between each layer. After the layers are stacked, spread buttercream over the entire cake and rim the top with malted milk balls.

COOKIES AND CREAM CAKE

Chocolate Cake:
1 box devil's food cake mix
1 3.4- to 3.9-oz. pkg. chocolate instant pudding mix
4 eggs
¾ C. milk
¾ C. oil
1 C. sour cream
2 tsp. vanilla extract

Cream Cheese Frosting:
1 C. butter, softened
16 oz. cream cheese
1 T. vanilla extract
2 T. milk
5–6 C. powdered sugar
2 C. chocolate cream cookies, crushed

Decoration:
Chocolate cream sandwich cookies, crushed
Chocolate cream sandwich cookies, whole
Melted chocolate

1. Preheat oven to 350 degrees and grease three 8-inch pans. (You can make this cake with only two layers; see baking time below.) I like to use foil or parchment paper to line the bottoms of my pans for easy cleanup and removal.
2. Sift cake mix and instant pudding mix into a small bowl; set aside.
3. In a large bowl, combine eggs, milk, oil, sour cream, and vanilla extract.
4. Stir in cake mix and instant pudding mix.
5. Divide batter between prepared pans and use a spatula to spread the batter evenly.
6. Bake for 17–22 minutes or until a knife inserted near the center comes out clean. (If you are making only two layers, bake for 20–25 minutes.)
7. Let cake cool completely.
8. Cream Cheese Frosting: Beat butter and cream cheese. Add vanilla extract and milk; gradually add powdered sugar until frosting reaches the desired consistency.
9. Place roughly ⅓ of the frosting into a small bowl with the 2 C. crushed chocolate cream sandwich cookies and fold until combined. This will be the frosting you use between your cake layers.
10. To assemble the cake, stack the layers, frosting between each layer as you stack. Cover the entire cake with cream cheese frosting that has not been mixed with the crushed cookies. Decorate with cookies, crushed cookies, and melted chocolate.

STRAWBERRY VANILLA CAKE

Very Vanilla Cake:

1 box white cake mix
3 eggs
⅓ C. oil
1 C. milk
½ C. plain yogurt or sour cream
1 T. vanilla extract

Strawberry Buttercream:

2½ C. butter, softened
⅓ C. pureed* strawberries
2 tsp. vanilla extract
6–7 C. powdered sugar

Strawberries for decoration

1. Preheat oven to 350 degrees and grease three 8-inch pans. (You can make this cake with only two layers; see baking time below.) I like to use foil or parchment paper to line the bottoms of my pans for easy cleanup and removal.
2. Sift cake mix into a small bowl; set aside.
3. In a large bowl, combine eggs, oil, milk, yogurt, and vanilla extract until smooth.
4. Stir in cake mix.
5. Divide batter between prepared pans and use a spatula to spread batter evenly.
6. Bake for 17–22 minutes or until a knife inserted near the center comes out clean. (If you are making only two layers, bake for 20–25 minutes.)
7. Let cake cool completely.
8. Strawberry Buttercream: Beat butter for 2 minutes. Add roughly half of the pureed strawberries. Stir in vanilla extract; gradually add powdered sugar until buttercream becomes slightly thicker than desired. Stream in more strawberry puree until buttercream reaches the desired consistency. (You might not use all the puree.)
9. Assemble the cake, frosting between each layer and covering the entire cake with the remaining buttercream. Top with fresh berries for decoration.

*Puree strawberries in a blender; measure after they are pureed. To get a more vibrant color and stronger taste, use freeze-dried strawberries. Pulverize them in a food processor and beat into buttercream in place of puree.

ROCKY ROAD CAKE

Chocolate Cake:
1 box devil's food cake mix
3 eggs
½ C. oil
1 C. milk
½ C. plain yogurt or sour cream
2 tsp. vanilla extract
1½ C. mini chocolate chips

Chocolate Buttercream:
2½ C. butter, softened
¾ C. unsweetened cocoa powder
2 tsp. vanilla extract
¼ C. milk or sour cream
5–6 C. powdered sugar

Ganache:
½ C. chocolate chips
½ C. heavy whipping cream

2 C. marshmallows
2 C. walnuts
½ C. chopped chocolate or chocolate chips

1. Preheat oven to 350 degrees and grease three 8-inch pans. (You can make this cake with only two layers; see baking time below.) I like to use foil or parchment paper to line the bottoms of my pans for easy cleanup and removal.
2. Sift cake mix into a small bowl; set aside.
3. In a large bowl, combine eggs, oil, milk, yogurt, and vanilla extract until smooth.
4. Stir in cake mix and chocolate chips.
5. Divide batter between prepared pans and use a spatula to spread batter evenly.
6. Bake for 17–22 minutes or until a knife inserted near the center comes out clean. (If you are making only two layers, bake for 20–25 minutes.)
7. Let cake cool completely.
8. Chocolate Buttercream: Beat butter for 2 minutes. Add cocoa, vanilla extract, and milk; beat again. Gradually add powdered sugar until buttercream reaches desired consistency.
9. Ganache: In a microwave-safe bowl, combine chocolate chips and heavy whipping cream; heat for 40 seconds. Stir and continue to heat in 10-second increments until smooth.
10. To assemble the cake, stack layers; on each layer, spread chocolate buttercream, sprinkle marshmallows and walnuts onto the buttercream layer, and press the marshmallows and walnuts gently into the buttercream with your fingers. Repeat with the next layer. Stack the final layer onto the cake. Cover the entire cake with buttercream. Pour warm ganache slowly over the cake and let set. Cover the cake with extra marshmallows, walnuts, and chopped chocolate.

BANANA PEANUT BUTTER CAKE

Banana Cake:
1 box white or yellow cake mix
2 bananas, ripe and mashed
3 eggs
⅓ C. oil
1 C. sour cream
2 tsp. vanilla extract
1½ C. chocolate chips

Peanut Butter Buttercream:
1½ C. butter, softened
1 C. peanut butter
¼ C. sour cream or milk
1 T. vanilla extract
5–6 C. powdered sugar

Peanuts, banana slices, and chopped chocolate for decoration

1. Preheat oven to 350 degrees and grease three 8-inch pans. (You can make this cake with only two layers; see baking time below.) I like to use foil or parchment paper to line the bottoms of my pans for easy cleanup and removal.
2. Sift cake mix into a small bowl; set aside.
3. In a large bowl, combine bananas, eggs, oil, sour cream, and vanilla extract.
4. Stir in cake mix and chocolate chips.
5. Divide batter between prepared pans and use a spatula to spread the batter out evenly.
6. Bake for 17–22 minutes or until a knife inserted near the center comes out clean. (If you are making only two layers, bake for 20–25 minutes.)
7. Let cake cool completely.
8. Peanut Butter Buttercream: Beat butter and peanut butter. Add sour cream and vanilla extract; beat again. Gradually add powdered sugar until buttercream reaches desired consistency. If it becomes too thick or dry, add more sour cream/milk.
9. To assemble the cake, stack layers, frosting between each layer. Cover the entire cake with the remaining buttercream. Decorate with peanuts, banana slices, and chopped chocolate.

LEMON BERRY CAKE

Lemon Cake:
1 box white cake mix
3 eggs
⅓ C. melted butter, cooled
Zest of 2 lemons
⅓ C. lemon juice
⅔ C. buttermilk or milk
½ C. plain yogurt or sour cream
2 C. blueberries, fresh or frozen

Raspberry Buttercream:
½ C. butter, softened
8 oz. cream cheese
2 T. raspberry puree (pureed in blender), strained to remove seeds*
3½–4½ C. powdered sugar

Lemon Buttercream:
1 C. butter, softened
8 oz. cream cheese
Zest of 2 lemons
1 T. lemon juice
3½–4½ C. powdered sugar

Fresh raspberries for decoration

1. Preheat oven to 350 degrees and grease three 8-inch pans. (You can make this cake with only two layers; see baking time below.) I like to use foil or parchment paper to line the bottoms of my pans for easy cleanup and removal.
2. Sift cake mix into a small bowl; set aside.
3. In a large bowl, combine eggs, butter, lemon zest, lemon juice, buttermilk, and yogurt until smooth.
4. Stir in cake mix and blueberries.
5. Divide batter between prepared pans and use a spatula to spread batter evenly.
6. Bake for 17–22 minutes or until a knife inserted near the center comes out clean. (If you are making only two layers, bake for 20–25 minutes.)
7. Let cake cool completely.
8. Raspberry Buttercream: Beat butter and cream cheese for 2 minutes. Stir in pureed raspberries; gradually add powdered sugar until the buttercream reaches desired consistency.
9. Lemon Buttercream: Beat butter, cream cheese, and lemon zest. Stir in lemon juice; gradually add powdered sugar until the buttercream reaches desired consistency.
10. To assemble the cake, stack the layers, spreading the raspberry buttercream between each layer. Cover the entire cake with lemon buttercream. Top with fresh berries.

*Note: As an alternate, you can use freeze-dried raspberries in the buttercream. Pulverize them in a food processor and then sift out the seeds. Use about 1 T. pulverized berries for an amazing punch of color and flavor. OR you can add 3 tsp. raspberry-flavored gelatin to the original recipe for extra color and flavor.

SNICKERDOODLE CAKE

Snickerdoodle Cake:
1 box yellow or white cake mix
1 T. cinnamon
4 eggs
⅔ C. melted butter, cooled
⅔ C. milk or buttermilk
1 C. sour cream
1 T. vanilla extract
1 3.4- to 3.9-oz. pkg. vanilla instant pudding mix

Snickerdoodle Buttercream:
1½ C. butter, softened
8 oz. cream cheese
¼ C. sour cream or milk
3 tsp. vanilla extract
5–6 C. powdered sugar

Cinnamon and sugar for decoration

1. Preheat oven to 350 degrees and grease two 9-inch round pans. I like to use foil or parchment paper to line the bottom of my pans for easy cleanup and removal.
2. Sift cake mix and cinnamon into a small bowl; set aside.
3. In a large bowl, combine eggs, butter, milk, sour cream, and vanilla extract until smooth.
4. Stir in cake mix, cinnamon, and pudding mix.
5. Divide batter between prepared pans and use a spatula to spread batter evenly.
6. Bake for 20–25 minutes or until a knife inserted near the center comes out clean.
7. Let cake cool completely.
8. Snickerdoodle Buttercream: Beat butter and cream cheese for 2 minutes. Stir in sour cream and vanilla extract; gradually add powdered sugar until buttercream reaches desired consistency.
9. Assemble cake by frosting between each layer and then frosting the entire cake. Decorate with cinnamon sugar.

LEMON RASPBERRY WHIPPED CREAM CAKE

Lemon Cake:

1 box white cake mix

3 eggs

⅓ C. oil

Zest of 2 lemons

¼ C. lemon juice

½ C. buttermilk or milk

½ C. plain yogurt

1 tsp. vanilla extract

Raspberry Whipped Cream Filling:

2 C. heavy whipping cream

1 3.4- to 3.9-oz. pkg. instant white chocolate pudding mix

⅓ C. raspberries, coarsely chopped

Extra raspberries for decoration

1. Preheat oven to 350 degrees and grease three 8-inch round pans. I like to use foil or parchment paper to line the bottoms of my pans for easy cleanup and removal.
2. Sift cake mix into a small bowl; set aside.
3. In a large bowl, combine eggs, oil, lemon zest, lemon juice, buttermilk, yogurt, and vanilla extract until smooth.
4. Stir in cake mix.
5. Divide batter between pans and use a spatula to spread batter evenly. Bake for 17–22 minutes or until a knife inserted in the center comes out clean.
6. Let cool and level the cakes, if desired, by carefully cutting off the rounded top.
7. Raspberry Whipped Cream Filling: Using a whisk attachment, whip cream and pudding mix on high until stiff peaks form. Fold in chopped raspberries for color and flavor.
8. To assemble, place a layer of cake on a plate. Top with ⅓ of the filling and spread evenly. Continue with the other two layers of cake. Decorate the top with extra raspberries.
9. Put the cake in the freezer for 10 minutes before cutting it so it will be easier to cut.

Cookies

    Imagine an island in the middle of a river, with fields and fields of pumpkins—complete with their twisty vines and dark green leaves—as far as you can see.

    Welcome to Sauvie Island.

    There are hayrides, corn mazes, pony rides, tractors to climb on, and booths full of autumn treats. As a kid, I couldn't have dreamed of a better place to start the spooky season. The whole island smells of apple cider and pumpkin spice, and the fog over the river makes you feel like you're on a hidden island. We'd trek out to the middle of the field, find the biggest pumpkin each of us could carry, cut the stems free, and head home to carve. Maybe it's the Oregon pride in me, but there's no better way to explore a pumpkin patch than in a rain jacket and muddy boots.

PEANUT BUTTER CHOCOLATE CHIP PUMPKIN COOKIES

Yields about 20 cookies

1 box white cake mix (can use spice cake mix; just omit pumpkin pie spice)
1 T. pumpkin pie spice
15 oz. pumpkin puree
½ C. butter, melted
1 C. mini chocolate chips
1 C. peanut butter chips

1. Preheat oven to 350 degrees and line cookie sheets with parchment paper.
2. In a large bowl, combine cake mix, pumpkin pie spice, pumpkin, and butter until smooth.
3. Stir in chocolate chips and peanut butter chips.
4. Scoop out dough balls about the size of a golf ball. Gently press down on each dough ball because cake mix cookies tend to get too tall while baking. (The dough is quite sticky, so put a little water on your fingertips before pressing down on the dough.)
5. Bake for 12–14 minutes.
6. Let cool and enjoy!

Tip: After I scoop out the batter and flatten the cookies a little bit, I push a few extra chocolate chips and peanut butter chips into each dough ball so a lot of chips are showing on the baked cookies.

CHOCOLATE CRINKLES COOKIES

Yields about 20 cookies

1 box devil's food cake mix
3 T. brown sugar
⅓ C. oil
2 eggs
2 tsp. vanilla extract
½ C. powdered sugar

1. Preheat oven to 350 degrees and line cookie sheets with parchment paper.
2. Sift cake mix into a large bowl to remove lumps. Add brown sugar, oil, eggs, and vanilla extract; stir until smooth.
3. Roll dough in your hands to make smooth balls; drop each ball into powdered sugar to coat evenly. Place dough balls on cookie sheets 2 inches apart. Press down on each cookie slightly because cake mix cookies tend to get too tall while baking.
4. Bake for 8–12 minutes.
5. Let cool and enjoy!

BANANA SPLIT COOKIES

Yields about 20 cookies

1 box white cake mix
1 3.4- to 3.9-oz. pkg. banana instant pudding mix
2 eggs
½ C. oil
1 tsp. vanilla extract
½ C. chocolate chips
½ C. maraschino cherries, chopped
¼ C. sprinkles

1. Preheat oven to 350 degrees and line cookie sheets with parchment paper.
2. Sift cake mix and pudding mix into a large bowl.
3. Add eggs, oil, and vanilla extract; stir until smooth. Dough will be thick.
4. Stir in chocolate chips.
5. Gently fold in cherries and sprinkles. (If desired, you can use a confetti cake mix and skip the sprinkles.)
6. Scoop out dough balls a little smaller than the size of a golf ball and place on a cookie sheet 2–3 inches apart. Gently press down on the top of each dough ball because cake mix cookies tend to get too tall while baking.
7. Bake for 9–11 minutes.
8. Let cool.

CHOCOLATE CHIP COOKIES

Yields about 20 cookies

1 box yellow cake mix
2 eggs
½ C. butter, softened
2 T. brown sugar
1 tsp. vanilla extract
1½ C. chocolate chips

1. Preheat oven to 350 degrees and line cookie sheets with parchment paper.
2. Sift cake mix into a large bowl to remove any lumps; add eggs, butter, brown sugar, and vanilla extract. Stir until combined.
3. Mix in chocolate chips.
4. Make 1½-T. dough balls and place on cookie sheets 2 inches apart. Gently press down on the top of each dough ball because cake mix cookies tend to get too tall while baking.
5. Bake for 8–12 minutes.
6. Let cool and enjoy!

ULTIMATE GRASSHOPPER COOKIES

Yields about 20 cookies

Cookies:
1 box devil's food cake mix
2 eggs
⅓ C. butter, melted
1 tsp. vanilla extract
2 T. brown sugar

Mint Frosting:
¾ C. butter, softened
1½ tsp. peppermint extract
2–3 C. powdered sugar
Milk, if needed
Green food dye (optional)

Chocolate Glaze:
1½ C. chocolate chips
3 T. butter

Andes mint candies, roughly chopped

1. Preheat oven to 350 degrees and line cookie sheets with parchment paper.
2. Combine cake mix, eggs, butter (cool it a little so it doesn't cook the eggs), vanilla extract, and brown sugar. The batter will be stiff.
3. Make dough balls a little larger than a tablespoon and place on cookie sheets to bake. Press each dough ball down slightly because cake mix cookies tend to get too tall while baking.
4. Bake for 7–9 minutes and cool on cooling racks.
5. Mint Frosting: Beat butter for 2 minutes. Add peppermint extract; slowly add powdered sugar until the frosting reaches the desired consistency. Add 1–2 T. milk if the frosting gets too thick. Add green food dye for color if desired.
6. Chocolate Glaze: In a microwave-safe bowl, combine chocolate chips and butter; heat for about 30 seconds, then stir. Heat in 10-second increments and stir until smooth.
7. To assemble, pipe on frosting, smooth frosting with a knife, spoon glaze over frosting, and top with mint candies. (See photos.)

COOKIES AND CREAM COOKIES

Yields about 20 cookies

1 box white cake mix
½ C. melted butter, cooled
1 egg
1½ tsp. vanilla extract
1 C. chocolate cream cookies, chopped

1. Preheat oven to 350 degrees and line cookies sheets with parchment paper.
2. In a large bowl, combine cake mix, butter, egg, and vanilla extract until smooth.
3. Stir in chopped cookies.
4. Make dough balls slightly larger than 1½ inches in diameter; place on cookie sheet 3 inches apart. Gently press down on each dough ball because cake mix cookies tend to get too tall while baking.
5. Bake for 11–14 minutes.
6. Let cool and serve with milk.

CHOCOLATE CANDY CANE COOKIES

Yields about 20 cookies

Chocolate Cookies:
1 box devil's food cake mix
⅓ C. oil
2 eggs
2 T. brown sugar
1 tsp. vanilla extract
1 tsp. peppermint extract
1 C. mini chocolate chips

White chocolate, melted, for decoration
Crushed candy canes for decoration

1. Preheat oven to 350 degrees and line cookie sheets with parchment paper.
2. In a large bowl, combine cake mix, oil, eggs, brown sugar, vanilla extract, and peppermint extract. The dough will be quite thick.
3. Stir in chocolate chips.
4. Scoop into walnut-sized balls and place on cookie sheets 2 inches apart. Gently press down each dough ball so that the cookies don't get too tall while baking.
5. Bake for 8–10 minutes (8 for a fudge-like cookie and 10 for a cake-like cookie).
6. Let cool.
7. Drizzle or pipe melted white chocolate over cookies and top immediately with crushed candy canes.

SNICKERDOODLES

Yields about 20 cookies

1 box white or yellow cake mix
½ C. butter, melted
1 egg
1 tsp. vanilla extract
2 T. sugar
1 tsp. cinnamon

1. Preheat oven to 350 degrees and line cookie sheets with parchment paper.
2. In a large bowl, combine cake mix, butter, egg, and vanilla extract until smooth.
3. In a small bowl, combine sugar and cinnamon. (Feel free to add more cinnamon if desired.)
4. Scoop dough into balls about the size of a golf ball; roll in cinnamon-sugar mixture and place on cookie sheets. Gently press down on each dough ball because cake mix cookies tend to get too tall while baking.
5. Bake for 9–12 minutes and let cool.

EGGNOG COOKIES

Yields about 20 cookies

1 box white cake mix
½ tsp. nutmeg
½ C. melted butter, cooled
3 eggs
¼ C. eggnog

Eggnog Glaze:
2 T. eggnog
1 pinch nutmeg
1–2 C. powdered sugar

1. Preheat oven to 350 degrees and line cookie sheets with parchment paper.
2. In a large bowl, combine cake mix, nutmeg, butter, eggs, and eggnog until smooth.
3. Scoop dough balls slightly smaller than golf balls onto the cookie sheets, placing them 2 inches apart. Gently press down on each dough ball because cake mix cookies tend to get too tall while baking.
4. Bake for 9–12 minutes; let cool.
5. Eggnog Glaze: In a medium bowl, use a fork or whisk to combine eggnog, nutmeg, and 1 C. powdered sugar. Depending on how thick or runny you want the glaze, add either more powdered sugar or eggnog.
6. Glaze cooled cookies. Go heavy on the glaze, because that's where you get most of the eggnog flavor!

KEY LIME PIE COOKIES

Yields about 20 cookies

Lime Curd:
1 C. sugar
¼ C. butter
¾ C. fresh lime juice
1 T. lime zest
1 tsp. flour
2 eggs, lightly beaten

Lime Cookies:
1 box white cake mix
3 eggs
½ C. melted butter, cooled
Zest of 2 limes

1. Lime Curd: In a small saucepan, combine sugar, butter, lime juice, lime zest, and flour; heat over medium heat until butter melts. Pour 2 T. of hot lime mixture into the beaten eggs to temper them. Then whisk eggs into lime mixture on stove. Cook until mixture is thickened and coats the back of a wooden spoon. Remove from heat and let cool.
2. Lime Cookies: Combine cake mix, eggs, butter, and lime zest until smooth.
3. Scoop dough balls about the size of golf balls onto your cookie sheets. Gently press down on each dough ball because cake mix cookies tend to get too tall while baking.
4. Bake for 8–11 minutes.
5. Remove from oven; as soon as the cookies are cool enough to touch, press your thumb into each cookie to make an indent for the filling.
6. Once the cookies have cooled, fill the indentations with filling. Go heavy on the filling, because it's the BEST part of the cookie!

Note: To make lemon-lime cookies, use lemon zest to make lemon curd, or use a lemon cake mix to make the cookies.

CHOCOLATE TRAIL MIX COOKIES

Yields about 20 cookies

1 box devil's food cake mix
2 eggs
½ C. oil
2 tsp. vanilla extract
1 T. brown sugar
⅓ C. peanuts
⅓ C. chocolate candies
⅓ C. dried cranberries

1. Preheat oven to 350 degrees and line cookie sheets with parchment paper.
2. In a large bowl, combine cake mix, eggs, oil, vanilla extract, and brown sugar until smooth.
3. Stir in peanuts, chocolate candies, and dried cranberries.
4. Scoop out dough balls the size of golf balls and place on cookie sheets 2 inches apart. Gently press down on each dough ball with your fingertips because cake mix cookies tend to get too tall while baking.
5. Bake for 8–10 minutes, let cool, and hit the trail!

LEMON COOKIES

Yields about 20 cookies

1 box lemon cake mix
2 eggs
⅓ C. oil
1 T. lemon juice
Zest of 1 lemon
⅓ C. sugar

1. Preheat oven to 350 degrees and line cookie sheets with parchment paper.
2. In a large bowl, combine cake mix, eggs, oil, lemon juice, and lemon zest until smooth.
3. Scoop dough balls about the size of a golf ball and roll each in sugar.
4. Place on cookie sheets 2 inches apart, gently press down with your fingertips, and bake for 7–9 minutes.
5. Let cool and enjoy!

Whoopie Pies

"Too much—it's too much!" This is always my father's reply to any dessert I make as he scrapes part of it down the kitchen sink—too much frosting or too much filling; too fudgey and not cakey enough; and never, ever enough nuts. My best friends and boyfriends will always say it's perfect, but I can count on my father to tell me the truth. The closest I ever get to pleasing his persnickety taste buds is when I bake up something German chocolate.

GERMAN CHOCOLATE WHOOPIE PIES

Yields 24 cookies,
12 whoopie pies

German Chocolate Filling:
½ C. evaporated milk
½ C. sugar
2 egg yolks, lightly beaten
¼ C. butter
1 tsp. vanilla extract
¾ C. chopped pecans
¾ C. flaked coconut

Chocolate Cookies:
1 box devil's food or German chocolate cake mix
2 eggs
⅓ C. oil
3 T. brown sugar
2 tsp. vanilla extract

1. German Chocolate Filling: In a saucepan, combine evaporated milk, sugar, egg yolks, and butter. Cook, stirring constantly, over medium-high heat until the mixture boils and thickens.
2. Remove from heat and stir in vanilla extract, pecans, and coconut.
3. Place in the refrigerator to help cool it more quickly and to keep it fresh until the cookies are done.
4. Chocolate Cookies: Preheat oven to 350 degrees and line cookie sheets with parchment paper.
5. Sift cake mix into a large bowl to remove any lumps.
6. Add eggs, oil, brown sugar, and vanilla extract; stir until smooth.
7. Make small dough balls and place 2 inches apart from each other on cookie sheets. Press down slightly with fingertips before baking.
8. Bake for 8–10 minutes.
9. Let cool.
10. To assemble, place a spoonful of chilled frosting on the bottom of a cooled cookie. Place an unfrosted cookie on top of the frosted cookie and press gently to secure the "sandwich." Repeat with remaining cookies.

BROWNIE CREAM WHOOPIE PIES

Yields 22 cookies,
11 whoopie pies

Brownie Cookies:
1 box devil's food cake mix
2 eggs
⅓ C. oil
1½ tsp. vanilla extract

Cream Cheese Filling:
4 oz. cream cheese, softened
¼ C. butter, softened
1½–2½ C. powdered sugar
1 tsp. vanilla extract

1. Preheat oven to 350 degrees and line cookie sheets with parchment paper.
2. In a medium bowl, mix cake mix, eggs, oil, and vanilla extract; the dough will be thick.
3. Line cookie sheets with parchment paper. Form dough balls smaller than the size of golf balls.
4. Place dough balls on cookie sheets, about 12 per sheet, and use your fingertips to lightly press down the tops.
5. Bake for 6–9 minutes; be careful not to overbake.
6. Let cool on cookie sheets for 1 minute and then gently move to cooling racks.
7. Cream Cheese Filling: Beat cream cheese and butter for 3 minutes. Add powdered sugar and vanilla extract. Thicken with more powdered sugar if needed.
8. Once the cookies have cooled, frost the bottoms of half the cookies and use the unfrosted cookies to make sandwiches.
9. Place cookies in an airtight container and chill for at least an hour in the refrigerator. Chilling keeps the filling from gushing out when you bite into them.

RED VELVET WHOOPIE PIES

Yields 24 cookies,
12 whoopie pies

Red Velvet Cookies:
1 box red velvet cake mix
2 eggs
⅓ C. oil
1½ tsp. vanilla extract
½ C. granulated sugar (use powdered sugar if you want the "crinkle" look)

Cream Cheese Filling:
4 oz. cream cheese, softened
¼ C. butter, softened
1 tsp. vanilla extract
3–4 C. powdered sugar

Coarse sugar or sprinkles for decoration

1. Preheat oven to 375 degrees and line cookie sheets with parchment paper.
2. In a large bowl, combine cake mix, eggs, oil, and vanilla extract.
3. Scoop out pieces of dough that are about 1 T. in size, or a little bigger. The dough will be gooey.
4. Drop each piece of dough into sugar and roll the dough until covered, forming a ball. Place balls on the cookie sheet 3 inches apart. Press down gently with your fingertips.
5. Bake for 6–10 minutes and let cool.
6. Cream Cheese Filling: Beat cream cheese and butter until smooth. Add vanilla extract and gradually add powdered sugar until the filling reaches the desired consistency.
7. Pipe filling onto the bottom of half the cookies, sandwich with another cookie, and roll the frosting rim in coarse sugar or colored sprinkles to decorate.

SNICKERDOODLE PEANUT BUTTER WHOOPIE PIES

Yields 24 cookies,
12 whoopie pies

Snickerdoodles:
1 box white cake mix
½ C. melted butter, cooled
1 egg
1 tsp. vanilla extract
2 T. sugar
1 tsp. cinnamon

Peanut Butter Frosting:
½ C. butter
⅓ C. peanut butter
1 tsp. vanilla extract
2 T. milk
2–3 C. powdered sugar

1. Preheat oven to 350 degrees and line cookie sheets with parchment paper.
2. In a medium bowl, combine cake mix, butter, egg, and vanilla extract.
3. In a separate bowl, combine sugar and cinnamon.
4. Form dough into balls about 1½ inches in diameter; roll each ball in cinnamon-sugar mixture.
5. Place dough balls on cookie sheets 2–3 inches apart.
6. Bake for 11–14 minutes. Let cool.
7. Peanut Butter Frosting: In a large bowl, beat butter and peanut butter. Add vanilla extract, milk, and 2 C. powdered sugar. If the frosting is too stiff, add another tablespoon of milk; if it's not thick enough, add more powdered sugar.
8. Pipe frosting onto the bottoms of half the cookies, then top with an unfrosted cookie to create the whoopie pie.

PUMPKIN CHOCOLATE CHIP WHOOPIE PIES

Yields 30 cookies,
15 whoopie pies

Pumpkin Chocolate Chip Cake Cookies:
1 box spice cake mix
1½ tsp. pumpkin pie spice
15 oz. pumpkin puree
½ C. applesauce
1⅓ C. mini chocolate chips

Cream Cheese Filling:
8 oz. cream cheese
¼ C. butter, softened
2–3 C. powdered sugar
1 tsp. vanilla extract
½ tsp. cinnamon

1. Preheat oven to 350 degrees and line cookie sheets with parchment paper.
2. In a large bowl, combine cake mix and pumpkin pie spice.
3. Stir in pumpkin and applesauce; mix until combined.
4. Stir in chocolate chips.
5. Spoon golf ball-sized dough balls onto cookie sheets and bake for 11–14 minutes or until the tops are cooked.
6. Place on cooling racks and cool completely.
7. Cream Cheese Filling: Beat cream cheese and butter until smooth. Add powdered sugar, vanilla extract, and cinnamon. Beat for 2–3 minutes.
8. Assemble cookie sandwiches by piping or spooning filling onto the bottom side of half the cookies and placing unfrosted cookies on top.
9. Refrigerate cookies until chilled, about 1 hour. Not only do they taste better cold, but chilling them keeps the filling from gushing out when you bite into them.

OATMEAL WHOOPIE PIES

Yields 24 cookies,
12 whoopie pies

Oatmeal Cookies:

1 box white cake mix (or spice cake mix; omit added spices)
2 tsp. pumpkin pie spice
½ tsp. cinnamon
2 eggs
½ C. oil
⅓ C. applesauce, unsweetened
1½ T. brown sugar
2 C. quick oats

Brown Sugar Cream Filling:

4 oz. cream cheese, softened
¼ C. butter, softened
⅓ C. brown sugar
1 tsp. vanilla extract
2–4 C. powdered sugar

1. Preheat oven to 350 degrees and line cookie sheets with parchment paper.
2. Sift cake mix into a large bowl to remove any lumps.
3. Add pumpkin pie spice, cinnamon, eggs, oil, applesauce, and brown sugar; stir until combined.
4. Mix in quick oats.
5. Spoon tablespoon-sized dough balls onto cookie sheets 2 inches apart. Flatten slightly with fingertips and bake for 8–12 minutes.
6. Let cool.
7. Brown Sugar Cream Filling: Beat cream cheese, butter, and brown sugar for 2 minutes. Add vanilla extract; gradually add powdered sugar until the filling reaches the desired consistency.
8. To assemble, pipe frosting onto the bottom of half of the cookies, then place an unfrosted cookie on top to create a "sandwich."

CARROT CAKE WHOOPIE PIES

Yields 28 cookies,
14 whoopie pies

Carrot Cookies:
1 box white cake mix (or spice cake mix; omit pumpkin pie spice)
2 tsp. pumpkin pie spice
2 eggs
½ C. oil
1 tsp. vanilla extract
1¼ C. quick oats
¼ C. crushed pineapple (drain well before measuring)
1¼ C. carrots, shredded (3–4 large carrots)
½ C. raisins, optional
½ C. walnuts, optional

Cream Cheese Filling:
6 oz. cream cheese, softened
¼ C. butter, softened
1½ tsp. vanilla extract
2–4 C. powdered sugar

1. Preheat oven to 350 degrees and line cookie sheets with parchment paper.
2. Sift cake mix into a large bowl to remove any lumps.
3. Add pumpkin pie spice, eggs, oil, vanilla extract, quick oats, and crushed pineapple; stir until combined.
4. Stir in carrots, raisins, and walnuts.
5. Form dough into 1- or 1½-tablespoon-sized balls and place them 2 inches apart on the cookie sheets. Bake for 10–12 minutes. If cookies from the first batch are too tall after baking, pat the next batch of dough balls down with your fingers.
6. Let cool.
7. Cream Cheese Filling: Beat cream cheese and butter for 2 minutes. Add vanilla extract; gradually add powdered sugar until the filling reaches the desired consistency.
8. To assemble, frost the bottom of half of the cookies. Place the unfrosted cookies on top of the frosted ones to create cookie "sandwiches."

CHOCOLATE COCONUT WHOOPIE PIES

Chocolate Cookies:
1 box devil's food cake mix
2 eggs
⅓ C. butter, melted and cooled slightly
2 T. brown sugar
2 tsp. vanilla extract

Coconut Cream Filling:
4 oz. cream cheese, softened
¼ C. butter, softened
1½ tsp. coconut extract
3–4 C. powdered sugar

Shredded coconut for decoration

1. Preheat oven to 350 degrees and line cookie sheets with parchment paper.
2. Sift cake mix into a large bowl to remove any lumps.
3. Add eggs, butter, brown sugar, and vanilla extract; stir until combined well.
4. Form dough balls, each with 1 or 1½ T. dough (depending on how large you want the finished product to be); place the balls on the cookie sheets 2 inches apart. Gently pat down the cookies a little with your fingertips.
5. Bake for 7–12 minutes, depending on how fudge-like or cake-like you want the cookies to be.
6. Coconut Cream Filling: Beat cream cheese and butter for 2 minutes. Add coconut extract. Gradually add powdered sugar until the filling reaches the desired consistency.
7. To assemble, frost the bottom of half of cooled cookies. Place an unfrosted cookie on top of each frosted one, creating cookie "sandwiches." Roll exposed edges of filling in shredded coconut for added decoration.

DOUBLE CHOCOLATE PEANUT BUTTER WHOOPIE PIES

Chocolate Cookies:
1 box devil's food cake mix
2 eggs
½ C. butter, melted, then slightly cooled
3 T. brown sugar
2 tsp. vanilla extract
1⅓ C. peanut butter baking chips

Chocolate Peanut Butter Filling:
½ C. butter, softened
⅓ C. creamy peanut butter
⅓ C. unsweetened cocoa powder
2 tsp. vanilla extract
1–2 T. milk
2–3 C. powdered sugar

1. Preheat oven to 350 degrees and line cookie sheets with parchment paper.
2. Sift cake mix into a large bowl and add eggs, butter, brown sugar, and vanilla extract. Stir until combined.
3. Fold in peanut butter chips.
4. Form dough balls, each with 1 or 1½ T. dough, and place on the cookie sheets 2 inches apart. Gently press down the top of each dough ball with your fingertips.
5. Bake for 8–12 minutes.
6. Let cool.
7. Chocolate Peanut Butter Filling: Beat butter and peanut butter for 2 minutes. Add cocoa powder, vanilla extract, and 1 T. milk. Gradually add powdered sugar until the filling reaches the desired consistency. If it becomes too thick, add more milk.
8. To assemble, frost the bottom of half of the cookies. Top each with an unfrosted cookie to create cookie "sandwiches."

More to Crave

I grew up camping every summer. This was no pansy camping, either. No official campsites, no running water, no sign of civilization, and zero hope of any cell phone reception for days. Everything was always covered in dirt, and sleeping on the ground got rough after a while. But when it was time for dessert at the end of a long day, my grandmother made sure we always got the best. There was always a cobbler bubbling in her old Dutch oven over the hot coals. To this day, the aroma and flavor of a rich berry cobbler takes me back to those campsites and to the love of my grandmother.

RED VELVET S'MORES BARS

Graham Cracker Crust:
1½ C. graham crackers, crushed
6 T. butter, melted
1 T. sugar

Red Velvet Brownies:
1 box red velvet cake mix
¼ C. oil
2 T. butter, melted
⅓ C. milk
1 egg

2 C. marshmallows

1. Preheat oven to 350 degrees and prepare an 8 x 8 or 9 x 9 pan by greasing it or lining it with foil or parchment paper. (I like to line mine with foil and leave some hanging over the edge of the pan so that after the bars are baked I can use the overhanging foil as handles to lift out the dessert.)
2. Graham Cracker Crust: In a medium bowl, combine the crushed graham crackers, butter, and sugar. Press firmly into the bottom of the prepared pan.
3. Red Velvet Brownies: In a large bowl, combine cake mix, oil, butter, milk, and egg until smooth. Pour over graham cracker crust in pan.
4. Bake for 30–35 minutes or until the brownies are nearly set. Remove from the oven.
5. Top with marshmallows and put back in the oven under BROIL for about 1 minute. Watch carefully! They can burn very quickly, so be careful! I usually watch them while they're in the oven and take them out as soon as they turn the perfect golden brown.
6. Let cool; cut with a warm buttered knife.

DIRT DOUGHNUTS

Yields 10 doughnuts

Devil's Food Doughnuts:
2¾ C. devil's food cake mix
2 eggs
¾ C. buttermilk
2 T. butter, melted
1 tsp. vanilla extract

Chocolate Glaze:
¼ C. plus 2 tsp. unsweetened cocoa powder
½ tsp. vanilla extract
3 T. milk
1½ C. powdered sugar

20 chocolate sandwich cookies, crushed

1. Preheat oven to 425 degrees and grease a doughnut pan.
2. In a large bowl, combine cake mix, eggs, buttermilk, butter, and vanilla extract until smooth.
3. Pipe into the doughnut pan, filling each well ⅔ full. (If you don't have a piping bag, pour the batter into a plastic bag, snip off the corner of the bag, and use it to pipe the batter.)
4. Bake for 7–9 minutes or until a knife inserted into a doughnut comes out clean. Let cool in pan for 5 minutes and then turn out.
5. Chocolate Glaze: Combine cocoa powder, vanilla extract, milk, and powdered sugar until smooth. Use additional powdered sugar to make the glaze thicker or more milk to make it thinner.
6. Dip cooled doughnuts into the glaze and top with crushed sandwich cookies. You can also add gummy worms to really get a "dirt" feel!

RED VELVET PUPPY CHOW

5 C. square rice cereal
1 C. red velvet cake mix
½ C. powdered sugar
¾ C. white chocolate melts or chips
¼ C. chocolate melts or chips
2 oz. cream cheese, room temperature
1½ T. milk

2 C. Valentine's colored candies
Heart sprinkles for extra decoration

1. Measure out rice cereal and put it in a large bowl.
2. In a large plastic bag or plastic container with a lid, combine cake mix and powdered sugar. Set aside.
3. In a microwave-safe bowl, combine chocolates; heat in the microwave until melted. (You can also heat on the stovetop in a pan over low heat.) Stir every minute; be sure not to burn the chocolate. Stir until smooth.
4. Stir in cream cheese and milk (the chocolate will get thicker, but it's okay).
5. Pour chocolate over cereal and stir until coated.
6. Dump chocolate-coated cereal into the bag or container of powdered sugar and cake mix mixture. Shake thoroughly until all cereal is coated.
7. Dump onto a cookie sheet and let cool.
8. Mix with extra colorful candies and serve immediately!

Note: Store any uneaten portion in bags or containers in the refrigerator.

CAKE BATTER BROWNIES

Brownie Layer:
1 box brownie mix
2 eggs
⅔ C. oil
¼ C. milk

Cake Batter Swirl:
1⅔ C. yellow or white cake mix (approx. ½ box of cake mix)
1 egg
2 T. oil
¼ C. milk
2 T. sprinkles

3 T. extra sprinkles for decoration

1. Preheat oven to 350 degrees. Line a 9 x 13 pan with foil and leave some hanging over the sides to use as handles to help remove brownies later (see photo). Grease any exposed glass not covered by foil.
2. Brownies: In a large bowl, combine all ingredients and pour into prepared pan. Spread batter evenly.
3. Cake Batter Swirl: In a medium bowl, combine all ingredients until smooth.
4. Drop spoonfuls of Cake Batter Swirl onto the brownie layer (see photo). Continue until batter is all used.
5. Using a knife, cut through the batter in the brownie mix to make a swirl or marbleized pattern.
6. Pour the remaining sprinkles over the brownies for decoration.
7. Bake for 28–35 minutes; check halfway through. If the cake on top seems to be browning too quickly, cover with foil. Check doneness by inserting a knife into the middle of the brownies; if it comes out clean, the brownies are done. If you want your brownies to be gooey, the knife should come out with a little chocolate on it.
8. Let cool in the pan. When cooled, lift up on foil to remove from the pan and cut with a warm knife.

CAKE BATTER RICE CRISPY TREATS

4 T. butter
1 10-oz. bag mini marshmallows
2 tsp. vanilla extract
⅔ C. yellow cake mix, sifted to remove any lumps
5 C. rice crispy cereal
¼ C. multicolored sprinkles*

Extra sprinkles for decoration*

*The tiny round sprinkles tend to bleed color into the marshmallow, so try to use Jimmies—the sprinkles shaped like tiny sticks.

1. Grease a 9 x 13 pan.
2. In a large microwave-safe bowl, combine butter, marshmallows, and vanilla extract. Heat for 1 minute, remove, and stir. Continue to heat in 10-second increments until smooth.
3. Stir in cake mix.
4. Stir in rice cereal.
5. Stir in sprinkles just until dispersed (the dye from the sprinkles will bleed if you handle it too much).
6. Dump into prepared pan; use a spatula or buttered hands to press evenly into the pan.
7. Top with extra sprinkles and gently press the sprinkles into the treats while still warm.
8. Let cool.
9. Use a warm knife to cut.

DEVIL'S FOOD RICE CRISPY TREATS

3 T. butter
1 10-oz. bag mini marshmallows
1 tsp. vanilla extract
⅔ C. devil's food cake mix, sifted to remove lumps
6 C. rice crispy cereal

Chocolate Ganache:
2 C. chocolate chips (milk or semisweet)
⅔ C. heavy whipping cream

Chocolate sprinkles for decoration

1. Grease a 9 x 13 pan.
2. In a large microwave-safe bowl, combine butter, marshmallows, and vanilla extract. Microwave for 1 minute, remove, and stir. Continue to microwave in 10-second increments until smooth.
3. Stir in cake mix.
4. Stir in rice cereal.
5. Dump into prepared pan; use a spatula or buttered hands to press evenly into pan.
6. Chocolate Ganache: In a microwave-safe bowl, combine chocolate chips and heavy whipping cream. Heat in the microwave for 40 seconds. Remove, stir, and continue to microwave in 10-second increments until smooth. Pour over rice crispy treats and top with sprinkles.
7. Let cool.
8. Use a warm knife to cut.

CHOCOLATE WAFFLES

Yields 4–5 large waffles

Waffles:
1 box devil's food cake mix
3 eggs
½ C. melted butter, cooled
1 C. milk or buttermilk

Chocolate Glaze:
¼ C. plus 2 tsp. unsweetened cocoa powder
½ tsp. vanilla extract
3 T. milk
1½ C. powdered sugar

Extra sprinkles, whipped cream, and maraschino cherries with stems for decoration

1. Plug in a waffle iron and turn it on.
2. In a large bowl, combine cake mix, eggs, butter, and milk until smooth.
3. Spray hot waffle iron with nonstick cooking spray if needed.
4. Pour about ½ C. batter into the waffle iron, close, and cook until done. Repeat until all the waffle batter has been used.
5. Chocolate Glaze: In a medium bowl, combine cocoa powder, vanilla extract, milk, and powdered sugar. Add more milk if too thick.
6. Pour glaze onto warm waffles and top with sprinkles, whipped cream, and cherries.

RED VELVET DOUGHNUTS

2¾ C. red velvet cake mix
2 eggs
¾ C. buttermilk
2 T. butter, melted
1 tsp. vanilla extract

Glaze:
½ tsp. vanilla extract
3 T. milk
1¾ C. powdered sugar

Red sprinkles for decoration (optional)

1. Preheat oven to 425 degrees and grease a doughnut pan.
2. In a large bowl, combine cake mix, eggs, buttermilk, butter, and vanilla extract until smooth.
3. Pipe batter into the doughnut pan, filling each well ⅔ full. (If you don't have a piping bag, pour the batter into a plastic bag, snip off the corner, and use it to pipe the batter.)
4. Bake for 7–9 minutes or until a knife inserted into a doughnut comes out clean. Let cool in pan for 5 minutes and then turn out.
5. Glaze: In a medium bowl, combine vanilla extract, milk, and powdered sugar until smooth. Use additional powdered sugar to make the glaze thicker or more milk to make it thinner.
6. Dip cooled doughnuts in the glaze and top with red sprinkles if desired.

Note: You can use 3 oz. cream cheese, melted in the microwave, instead of milk in the glaze; glaze made with cream cheese will be an off-white color instead of pure white.

KEY LIME COOKIE BARS

Cookie Bars:
1 box yellow cake mix
1 3.4- to 3.9-oz. box instant vanilla pudding
¼ C. milk
¾ C. vegetable oil
2 eggs
1½ C. chocolate chips (I use half chocolate, half white chocolate)
2 T. sprinkles for color

Cheesecake Filling:
8-oz. pkg. cream cheese, softened
½ C. sugar
1 egg
¼ C. lime juice
Zest of 2 limes
2 T. flour

1. Preheat oven to 350 degrees and grease a 9 x 13 pan.
2. Cookie Bars: In a large bowl, combine cake mix, pudding mix, milk, oil, and eggs until smooth.
3. Stir in chocolate chips and sprinkles.
4. Press half of the dough into the bottom of the prepared pan.
5. Cheesecake Filling: In a stand mixer, beat cream cheese and sugar until smooth. Add egg, lime juice, lime zest, and flour; beat again. Scrape down the sides of the bowl as needed.
6. Pour cheesecake filling in pan over cookie layer.
7. Crumble the remaining cookie dough over the cheesecake filling.
8. Bake for 38–45 minutes.
9. Let cool and use a sharp knife to cut.

PUMPKIN PIE BARS

Crust:
1 box yellow cake mix
¾ C. melted butter, cooled
1 egg

Pumpkin Pie Filling:
29 oz. pumpkin puree
1 T. pumpkin pie spice
3 eggs
½ C. brown sugar
½ C. sugar
1 tsp. vanilla extract

Streusel Topping (optional):
1 C. brown sugar
1 C. flour
6 T. butter, melted

1. Preheat oven to 350 degrees and grease a 9 x 13 pan.
2. Crust: In a medium bowl, stir yellow cake mix, butter, and egg until smooth. Press into the bottom of the prepared pan.
3. Pumpkin Pie Filling: In a large bowl, combine pumpkin puree, pumpkin pie spice, eggs, brown sugar, sugar, and vanilla extract until smooth. Pour over crust.
4. Streusel Topping (if desired): In a medium bowl, combine brown sugar, flour, and butter; crumble over pumpkin pie filling.
5. Bake for 40–45 minutes or until a knife inserted in the center of the dish comes out clean.
6. Let cool. Serve with whipped cream and a sprinkle of cinnamon.

PEANUT BUTTER SWIRL BROWNIES

Brownies:
1 box devil's food cake mix
½ C. melted butter, cooled
1 T. oil
⅓ C. brown sugar
¼ C. milk
2 eggs
2 tsp. vanilla extract
1 C. mini chocolate chips

Peanut Butter Swirl:
⅓ C. peanut butter, smooth
1 T. powdered sugar

1. Preheat oven to 350 degrees and grease an 8 x 8 or 9 x 9 pan. (I like to line mine with foil and let it hang over the sides so that when the brownies are baked I can use the foil as handles to help remove the dessert.)
2. In a large bowl, combine cake mix, butter, oil, brown sugar, milk, eggs, and vanilla extract until smooth.
3. Stir in chocolate chips.
4. Dump into prepared pan; use a spatula to spread out evenly.
5. Peanut Butter Swirl: In a small microwave-safe bowl, heat peanut butter for about 15 seconds or until it's runny. Stir in powdered sugar.
6. Place several dollops of peanut butter onto brownie batter; use a knife to drag through the batter to create "swirls."
7. Bake for 18–22 minutes; be careful not to overbake the brownies.
8. Let cool and enjoy with milk.

APPLE CRISP

7 C. apples, peeled, cored, and sliced
¼ C. sugar
1½ tsp. cinnamon
¼ C. lemon juice

Topping:
1 box yellow cake mix
¾ C. brown sugar
¾ C. oats, quick or old-fashioned
½ C. butter, melted
1½ tsp. cinnamon

Ice cream

1. Preheat oven to 350 degrees and grease a 9 x 13 pan.
2. In a large bowl, gently fold apple slices, sugar, cinnamon, and lemon juice; dump into prepared pan.
3. Topping: In a large bowl, combine cake mix, brown sugar, oats, butter, and cinnamon. Crumble over apple slices and gently press down.
4. Bake for 45–50 minutes.
5. Serve warm with ice cream!

EASY BERRY COBBLER

Berry Cobbler:
5 C. berries, fresh or frozen (can use any kind of berries)
¼ C. sugar (optional)
1 box yellow cake mix
½ C. butter, melted
1 tsp. cinnamon (optional)

Egg white (optional)
Sugar, for sprinkling

1. Preheat oven to 350 degrees and lightly grease a 13 x 9 pan.*
2. Pour frozen or fresh berries into baking dish. If desired, fold ¼ C. sugar gently into berries before filling the pan; the sugar sweetens the berries and helps pull out the juices.
3. In a medium bowl, combine cake mix, melted butter, and cinnamon, if desired; stir until combined.
4. Crumble dough over berries.
5. Use a pastry brush to "paint" the egg white on top of the cobbler if desired. This is completely optional, but adds nice color. Sprinkle sugar on top to give a good crunch. (Note: You won't use the entire egg white.)
6. Bake for 28–35 minutes. You don't want to underbake a cobbler; the dough should be crispy.
7. Serve warm.

Note: You can also bake this cobbler in individual ramekins; this recipe fills about 9 ramekins.

Tips and Tricks

CAKE MIX SUBSTITUTIONS

Still not loving the cake mix idea? That's all right! Following are some cake mix substitution recipes. Simply mix the substitute up and use it in place of any recipe in this book where a cake mix is called for in the ingredient list.

CHOCOLATE CAKE MIX SUBSTITUTE

2 C. flour
1¾ C. sugar
¾ C. cocoa, unsweetened
2 tsp. baking powder
1 tsp. baking soda
½ tsp. salt
5 T. shortening

1. Using a food processor, combine all ingredients (the blades cut up the shortening and help blend it into the mixture).
2. Store in airtight plastic bags or jars until ready to use.
3. Use in place of chocolate cake mix in any recipe.

WHITE CAKE MIX SUBSTITUTE

2½ C. flour
1¾ C. sugar
1 T. baking powder
½ tsp. baking soda
¾ tsp. salt
½ C. powdered milk

1. Combine and sift all ingredients.
2. Seal in a plastic bag and use in place of any recipe calling for white cake mix.

BAKING TIMES

Mini Doughnuts:	Doughnuts:	Mini Cupcakes:	Cupcakes:	Mini Bundt Cakes:	Bundt Cake:	Three 8-inch pans:	Two 9-inch pans:
6–9 minutes	8–10 minutes	9–12 minutes	16–22 minutes	18–25 minutes	40–55 minutes	17–24 minutes	20–26 minutes

Note: Cakes using frozen fruit will take a few minutes longer to bake because the batter is cold.

CUTTING A RECIPE IN HALF:

If you want to use only half of a 15-oz. cake mix, you can!

I make small batches of cupcakes all the time because sometimes you just don't need 24 cupcakes. Simply pour out half the box of cake mix (just estimate—you don't have to measure) and continue with the recipe as directed, using only HALF of each ingredient listed. Most of my cake/cupcake recipes call for 3 eggs; if you're making a small batch, use 2 eggs (yes, I know 3 divided by 2 is not 2, but I promise it works). If the recipe calls for instant pudding mix, you can use half of the mix in the box OR you can omit the instant pudding mix altogether. If you eliminate the pudding mix, use only ¼ C. butter or oil (whichever the recipe calls for).

TRICKS TO GETTING "ROUND" TOPS ON YOUR CUPCAKES:

Sadly, sometimes what causes flat cupcakes is the oven. The heat in older ovens fluctuates, while newer ovens keep a constant temperature. I've baked the exact same recipes in different ovens, and the finished product always looks different in the end, so don't get discouraged. But I have discovered a few tricks that have worked for me.

- Let the batter rest for 25 minutes in your cupcake pan before baking.
- Heat your pan in the oven for a few minutes before putting in your liners, pouring in your batter, and baking.

CUPCAKE LINERS:

Do your colorful liners fade when they bake? To prevent fading, use greaseproof liners, available online or in specialty stores. I like to buy a few basic colors in bulk to cut down on prices because they are more expensive than normal liners. The liners that are lined with foil keep their color as well, but the foil often pulls away from the cupcakes. I always stick with the greaseproof liners just to be safe.

PICKING YOUR PIPING TIP:

There are three basic types of piping tips for cupcakes and cakes: open star, closed star, and circle. They all come in different sizes and give a very different look. The circle tip is the hardest to use because it doesn't hide any flaws. So if you're a beginner, start out with a star tip.

Tip Types

1. Open star—the triangles go straight out

2. Closed star—the triangles close into the center

3. Circle—this may look like it's the most simple but it is the most difficult tip to use because it shows every flaw

To practice your piping skills, use the bottom of a glass; the bottom of most glasses is about the size of a cupcake. You can pipe frosting onto the glass, scrape the frosting back into the bowl, and keep practicing until you feel like a pro!

HOW TO FILL A PIPING BAG:

- Slide the piping tip into the bag and push it into the hole until snug. Make sure the little triangles are not covered by the bag. If any are covered, remove the piping tip and use scissors to trim the bag.
- Turn the top of the bag inside out.
- Fill the bag with buttercream or frosting using either the cup method or the hand method.

  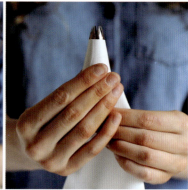

CUP METHOD

- Place the bag inside a tall glass or cup with the top of the bag hanging over the edge of the glass, inside out.
- Put a scoop full of frosting in the bag, using the edge of the glass to scrape off the frosting.
- Lift the bag from the glass and pull the top of the bag right-side out.
- Twist the bag right above where the frosting is; continue twisting to push the frosting down the inside of the bag until it starts to come out of the tip.

HAND METHOD

- Turn the bag inside out.
- Make a C shape with your hand then place your hand inside the bag.
- Use the side of your hand to scrape the frosting onto and into the bag.
- Once the bag is filled, turn the bag right side out and twist the bag right above the frosting.
- Continue twisting the bag to push the frosting down the inside of the bag until it starts to come out of the tip.

TIPS AND TRICKS • 181

FOOD SCOOPS:

I love my food scoops. Whenever I travel I take a piping bag, a piping tip, and a food scoop. It's an addiction, I know. But they save so much time and are a lot less messy than using a spoon/finger combination to get the batter into the pans. And when you're making cookies, scoops result in cookies that are all the same size and already rounded! What more could a baker ask for?

So what food scoop size is for you? Well, it depends on what you're baking.

Most food scoops are color-coded. For regular cupcakes, I like to use either a yellow (1⅝-oz.) or blue (2-oz.) scoop. For mini cupcakes I use a purple (¾-oz.) or black (1-oz.). And for cookies, I use a purple or black scoop for small cookies and a blue scoop for big cookies.

BUTTERCREAM BASICS:

Start with room-temperature butter in the mixer and beat for 2 minutes. (If the recipe calls for cream cheese, beat it with the butter.)

Stir in any flavorings and then gradually add the powdered sugar, 1 C. at a time. Keep adding the powdered sugar until the buttercream reaches the desired consistency.

For a cake, the buttercream needs to be easily spreadable. But for cupcakes, if you plan on piping the buttercream, it needs to be thick enough to stand on its own. To test it, cut through the buttercream with your finger and make sure the frosting doesn't move. You don't want it to sink back into itself. At the same time, don't make your frosting so thick that it takes a muscleman to pipe the frosting.

COMMON BUTTERCREAM MISTAKES:

- Make sure your butter has never been melted. Once it has been melted, you can't go back. Notice that when melted butter cools, it stays really yellow and never returns to the pale color it once was.
- Add enough powdered sugar. Depending on the temperature and where you live, the amount of powdered sugar you add will vary.
- Is it thick like cookie dough? Stream in a little milk to get a fluffy texture; as an alternate to milk, you can use sour cream or juice! The important part is to add more moisture.

REMOVING A BUNDT CAKE FROM THE PAN:

Once a Bundt cake has cooled completely, you're ready to turn it out. Follow these steps:

1. Place a serving plate, cake stand, or wire rack on top of the Bundt pan.
2. Use your hands to firmly hold the pan and wire rack/plate together.
3. Take a deep breath, lift the pan, and flip the pan on top of the wire rack/plate.

Remove the pan and admire your work!

DECIDING WHICH CAKE PANS TO USE:

The first thing you have to ask yourself is, "Do I want a tall and skinny cake or a short and wide cake?" Short cakes are usually easier to serve; as an added bonus, there is more space on top to decorate and fit lots of candles. But tall and skinny cakes have more layers and sometimes look more whimsical.

I love a three-layer cake baked with 8-inch pans because you get three layers but it's still manageable. Most people already have two 9-inch pans in their kitchen, so work with what you have!

LINING YOUR PANS:

Parchment paper is usually the best thing to use when lining a pan, but it can be a tad expensive. So I usually "cheat" and use aluminum foil. Just pull out a sheet and fold it to fit in the bottom of your cake pan. If you're making brownies or cookie bars, let the foil come up over the sides—then you can use the foil as "handles" to lift your brownies or treats out of the pan.

WHAT ABOUT "LEVELING" THE CAKES?

You can buy snazzy contraptions that will cut off the rounded part of the cake; you can also simply use a knife to cut it so you get that "flat" look. Honestly, I don't worry much about it. I figure, why cut off cake only to throw it away? It all depends on how you want your cake to look.

Depending on what size cake pans you use, you will get a bigger rise in the middle of your cake. The more batter you put in a pan, the bigger the rise will be.

You can usually still get that "flat-top look" by using extra frosting on top. If you do choose to cut the rounded part of the cake off, be careful that crumbs don't get in your frosting!

MAKING MORE LAYERS:

Do you have only two pans but want three or four layers in your cake? You have two options for solving your problem.

The first option is to bake the cake in two sessions. Using only part of the batter, bake the first two layers in the oven, let them cool, remove them from the pans, and use the same pans to bake the rest of the batter. The disadvantage with this method is that it takes a lot of extra time.

The second option, which saves time, is to bake all the batter in the two pans. When the cake has completely cooled, use a knife to cut each cake horizontally. If you want only three layers, bake ⅓ of the batter in one pan and ⅔ of the batter in the other. Once cool, cut only the thicker of the two cakes.

STACKING THE CAKE:

In stacking a cake, remember one important factor: gravity. You are trying to defy gravity by building a tall cake, so play by Mother Nature's rules.

No matter how perfectly you think you poured the batter into the pans, there is always a bigger cake and a smaller cake. So stack your cake layers with the biggest on the bottom. That way the heaviest layer is on the bottom.

When you frost between each layer, make sure the frosting creates a flat surface. Try not to have the frosting slant from one side to the other, because the cake you stack on top of it will slant too. As you're frosting, make sure the buttercream isn't too thin. Remember gravity: If the buttercream is too thin, it could gush out the sides when you put two more layers of cake on top. Relax; this doesn't happen too often, and is most common with berry fillings, but it's something to keep in mind.

FROSTING THE CAKE:

The number-one mistake in frosting a cake is not having enough frosting. It takes a decent amount to really get a professional look, so don't be stingy!

Your frosting should be spreadable but stiff enough that it does not slide off the cake. Carefully stack your cake and frost each layer all the way to the edge. Be generous with your frosting, because part of that "professional look" is having a nice layer of frosting between the layers of cake when you cut into it. Once your cake is stacked and frosted between the layers, it's time to cover the whole thing!

If you want to keep your plate really clean around the cake while you frost it, slip small pieces of parchment paper under your cake to protect the plate from getting messed up.

I like to start frosting the sides first. If you have a rotating cake stand, the process goes faster, but don't fret if you just use a simple cake plate. When you frost, fill in any irregularities so the sides are straight up and down—straight sides and a flat, smooth top make the cake look professional.

After the sides are covered, frost the top. Remember, use lots of frosting and get the top flat. You want that crisp edge when people look at your cake.

As far decorating your cake goes, keep it simple. In this book, I wanted to do only those things that an average person can do. I smother the sides with chocolate chips, pour ganache over the top and let it drip

down, top the cake with fresh fruit, or cover the cake in coconut or cookie crumbs. I haven't recommended fancy piping, fondant, or any other intricate details that are difficult to replicate. No matter your level of skill, you can make a beautiful cake.

CUTTING THE CAKE:

It's supposed to be a moment of glory when you cut into that cake you slaved away at. But sometimes cutting it ruins the cake because you can't seem to get that picture-perfect cut. The tricks? I'm glad you asked.
- Freeze the cake. Just five or ten minutes will do. This makes the frosting stiff enough that you can cut right through it instead of squishing it.
- Use a sharp, warm knife. Run your knife under warm water—warm, not hot. If the knife is too hot it will melt the frosting as it cuts through it. You just want it just warm enough to slip through the layers.
- Wipe off the knife. After every slice, wipe off the knife to continually get a clean cut.

FREQUENTLY ASKED QUESTIONS

Q. Why do you use cake mixes?
A. They help make baking simple and fast but still delicious! They are also great when it comes to guests who need gluten-free food—you simply use a gluten-free cake mix and you're set!

Q. Should I use salted or unsalted butter?
A. I use unsalted butter, but a lot of people prefer the taste of salted butter because it makes the dessert less sweet. It's completely up to you!

Q. My frosting won't get stiff enough. What am I doing wrong?
A. Check out my Buttercream Basics section on page 183 for all things buttercream!

Q. My cupcakes fall in the center; what can I do to fix that?
A. Try lowering the temperature of your oven to 325 degrees and extending the baking time by a few minutes. You can also play around with the rack level on which you bake your cupcakes.

Q. What about baking at high altitude?
A. One change I would make is filling the cupcake liners less to make sure they don't overflow. At high altitude, everything bakes faster too, so set your timer a few minutes less and check your treats early!

Q. I don't like cream cheese frosting; what can I use as a substitute?
A. For every 8 oz. of cream cheese, substitute ½ C. butter.

Q. How do you get your cookies and cupcakes such a uniform size?
A. Two of my favorite words: food scoops. Read all about them on page 182.

Q. What's your favorite piping tip?
A. I love the Wilton 2D tip, but I modify it, using a knife to open up the "prongs" a little more. When the prongs are too close, the piping tip gets clogged too easily. So I separate the prongs a little bit; I still get that beautiful, frilly look without any clogging mishaps!

Q. Is there any way to make a recipe healthier?
A. Of course, but sometimes you sacrifice taste. Greek yogurt in place of sour cream or yogurt adds extra protein. Applesauce used in place of butter or oil cuts down on fat. You can easily omit chocolate chips if the recipe calls for them. And you can always use less frosting!

Q. What kind of cupcake liners do you use? Mine lose all their color after I bake them!
A. Whenever I use a colored liner, I always make sure it's "greaseproof." You can find greaseproof liners in specialty stores or online. I like to buy a big stack of a color that I love online to save on costs.

Q. What's the best way to transport cakes and cupcakes?
A. Whenever possible, I wait to pipe my cupcakes until they are being served. It's much easier to transport plain cupcakes in a plastic container and bring my buttercream in the piping bag. When that's not an option, buy bakery boxes and pack them snugly into a plastic container so they don't slosh around on the drive. Another option is to put the cupcakes back into your cupcake pan; that keeps the cupcakes from bumping into each another. As for cakes, there are special cake carriers and cake boxes you can buy.

Q. Can I make a sheet cake with one of your recipes?
A. Of course! You can bake any size of cake you want using these recipes. Just adjust the baking time depending on the thickness of the cake.

Q. How long will cupcakes or a cake stay fresh?
A. I keep cakes or cupcakes in a container on the counter overnight if I'm serving them the next day. If it's any longer than that, I like to keep them in the freezer. The refrigerator dries cake out, so try to make room in your freezer instead! If possible, I always pipe cupcakes the day of the event to keep them as fresh as possible.

Q. What are your favorite recipes?
A. Black Forest Cupcakes
Brownie Cream Pies
Pumpkin Whoopie Pies
Carrot Cake Whoopie Pies
Banana Split Cookies
Chocolate Almond Raspberry Cupcakes
Chocolate Zucchini Bundt Cake
Blueberry Lemon Poppy Seed Bundt
Cake Batter Rice Crispy Treats
Easy Berry Cobbler

TIPS AND TRICKS • 189

INDEX

A

Almond blueberry Bundt cake, 39
Almond blueberry cake, 39
Almond buttercream, 30
Almond cherry cake, 30, 55
Andes Mint Cake, 75
Apple Crisp, 170

B

Baking times, 178
Banana Bundt with Chocolate Glaze and Walnuts, 48
Banana cake, 48, 92
Banana chocolate cake, 12
Banana cream filling, 12
Banana Peanut Butter Cake, 92
Banana Split Cookies, 107
Bars
    key lime cookie, 165
    pumpkin pie, 166
    red velvet s'mores, 149
Basics for buttercream, 183
Berry cobbler, 173
Birthday Bundt Cake, 63
Birthday Cake, 76
Black Forest Cupcakes, 3
Blackberry buttercream, 4
Blackberry Lemonade Cupcakes, 4
Blueberry almond cake, 39
Blueberry Almond Mini Bundt Cake, 39
Blueberry cinnamon cake, 33
Blueberry Cinnamon Toast Crunch™ Cupcakes, 33
Blueberry lemon poppy seed cake, 51
Breakfast Bundt Cake, 44
Brown sugar buttercream, 27
Brown sugar cream filling, 138
Brownie cookies, 130
Brownie Cream Whoopie Pies, 130
Brownies
    cake batter, 154
    peanut butter swirl, 169
    red velvet, 149
Bundt
    banana with chocolate glaze and walnuts, 48
    birthday, 63
    blueberry almond, 39
    breakfast, 44
    chocolate strawberry, 64
    chocolate zucchini, 40
    cinnamon swirl, 68
    cranberry orange, 71
    dark chocolate, 52
    hot chocolate, 47
    lemon blueberry poppy seed, 51
    mini cherry almond, 55
    orange cranberry, 71
    peaches and cream, 56
    pineapple with sweet strawberries, 60
    poppy seed lemon almond, 51
    pumpkin, 59
    raspberry lemonade, 67
    raspberry white chocolate, 43
    strawberry chocolate, 64
    zucchini chocolate, 40
Bundt cake, how to remove from pan, 184
Buttercream
    almond, 30
    basics, 183
    blackberry, 4
    brown sugar, 27
    cake batter, 76
    chocolate, 12, 15, 29, 91
    chocolate hazelnut, 79
    chocolate malt, 8, 84
    chocolate mint, 75
    Cinnamon Toast Crunch™, 33
    coconut, 83
    common mistakes, 184
    lemon, 95
    peanut butter, 92
    peppermint white chocolate chunk, 19
    raspberry, 95
    snickerdoodle, 96
    strawberry, 88
    white chocolate peppermint, 19

C

Cake Batter Brownies, 154
Cake batter buttercream, 76
Cake Batter Cupcakes, 16
Cake batter frosting, 16
Cake Batter Rice Crispy Treats, 157
Cake batter swirl, 154
Cake mix substitutions, 176
Cake pans, which to use, 184
Cake
    almond-cherry, 30
    Andes Mint, 75
    banana, 48, 92
    banana peanut butter, 92
    birthday, 76
    blueberry almond, 39
    blueberry cinnamon, 33
    cherry almond, 30, 55
    chocolate, 7, 8, 15, 19, 20, 47, 75, 79, 87, 91
    chocolate banana, 12
    chocolate buttermilk, 3
    chocolate chip, 80
    chocolate hazelnut, 78
    chocolate malt, 84
    chocolate raspberry, 29
    chocolate with strawberry swirl, 64
    chocolate zucchini, 40
    cinnamon blueberry, 33
    cinnamon blueberry buttermilk, 44
    coconut, 23
    confetti, 76

cookie dough, 80
cookies and cream, 87
cranberry orange, 71
dark chocolate, 52
Hawaiian vacation, 83
how to cut, 187
how to frost, 186
layers, 185
lemon, 67, 95, 98
lemon berry, 95
lemon blueberry poppy seed, 51
lemon raspberry whipped cream, 98
lemonade, 4
mango pineapple, 83
orange cranberry, 71
peach, 56
peanut butter banana, 92
pineapple, 11
pineapple mango, 83
pineapple upside-down, 60
pumpkin, 59
raspberry, 43
rocky road, 91
snickerdoodle, 96
stacking, 186
strawberry red velvet, 34
strawberry vanilla, 88
sweet potato, 27
vanilla, 68, 88
yellow, 63
yellow sprinkle, 16
zucchini chocolate, 40
Cakes, leveling, 185
Candy cane chocolate cookies, 115
Carrot Cake Whoopie Pies, 141
Carrot cookies, 141
Cheesecake filling, 165
Cherry almond cake, 55
Cherry almond mini Bundts, 55
Cherry filling, 3
Cherry glaze, 55
Chocolate almond ganache, 29
Chocolate Almond Raspberry Cupcakes, 29
Chocolate banana cake, 12
Chocolate Banana Cream Pie Cupcakes, 12
Chocolate buttercream, 12, 15, 29, 91

Chocolate buttermilk cake, 3
Chocolate cake, 7, 8, 15, 19, 20, 47, 75, 79, 87, 91
Chocolate cake mix substitution, 176
Chocolate cake with strawberry swirl, 64
Chocolate Candy Cane Cookies, 115
Chocolate chip cake, 80
Chocolate Chip Cookies, 108
Chocolate chip pumpkin cookies, 137
Chocolate chip pumpkin whoopie pies, 137
Chocolate Coconut Whoopie Pies, 142
Chocolate cookies, 129, 142, 145
Chocolate Crinkles Cookies, 104
Chocolate ganache, 3, 75, 158
Chocolate glaze, 48, 52, 64, 150, 161
Chocolate hazelnut buttercream, 79
Chocolate Hazelnut Cake, 79
Chocolate malt buttercream, 8, 84
Chocolate Malt Cake, 84
Chocolate mint buttercream, 75
Chocolate peanut butter filling, 145
Chocolate raspberry cake, 29
Chocolate Strawberry Bundt Cake, 64
Chocolate Trail Mix Cookies, 123
Chocolate waffles, 161
Chocolate Zucchini Bundt Cake, 40
Cinnamon blueberry buttermilk cake, 44
Cinnamon blueberry cake, 33
Cinnamon glaze, 40
Cinnamon Swirl Bundt Cake, 68
Cinnamon swirl, 68
Cinnamon Toast Crunch™ buttercream, 33
Cobbler, berry, 173
Coconut buttercream, 83

Coconut cake, 23
Coconut cream filling, 142
Coconut Lime Cupcakes, 23
Confetti cake, 76
Cookie Dough Cake, 80
Cookie dough frosting, 80
Cookies and Cream Cake, 87
Cookies and Cream Cookies, 112
Cookies
   banana split, 107
   brownie, 130
   carrot, 141
   chocolate, 129, 142, 145
   chocolate candy cane, 115
   chocolate chip pumpkin peanut butter, 103
   chocolate chip, 108
   chocolate crinkles, 104
   chocolate trail mix, 123
   cookies and cream, 112
   eggnog, 119
   grasshopper, 111
   key lime pie, 120
   lemon, 124
   lime, 120
   oatmeal, 138
   peanut butter chocolate chip pumpkin, 103
   pumpkin chocolate chip, 137
   pumpkin peanut butter chocolate chip, 103
   red velvet, 133
   snickerdoodles, 116
   trail mix, 123
Cranberry orange cake, 71
Cream cheese filling, 130, 133, 137, 141
Cream cheese frosting, 11, 34, 59, 87
Cream cheese glaze, 43, 56, 68
Creamy coconut filling, 83
Crisp, apple, 170
Crust, graham cracker, 27, 149
Cupcake liners, 179
Cupcakes
   almond raspberry chocolate, 29
   black forest, 3
   blackberry lemonade, 4
   blueberry Cinnamon Toast Crunch™, 33

cake batter, 16
cherry, 30
chocolate almond raspberry, 29
chocolate banana cream pie, 12
chocolate peanut butter, 20
Cinnamon Toast Crunch™, 33
coconut lime, 23
dirt, 15
double chocolate filled with sweet mascarpone, 8
getting round tops on, 178
maraschino cherry, 30
peanut butter chocolate, 20
peppermint bark, 19
pineapple cream, 11
raspberry white chocolate mousse, 24
red velvet strawberry, 34
s'mores, 7
strawberry red velvet, 34
sweet potato pie, 27
white chocolate raspberry, 24
Curd, lime, 120
Cutting a cake, 187
Cutting a recipe in half, 178

D

Dark Chocolate Bundt Cake, 52
Dark chocolate cake, 52
Devil's food doughnuts, 150
Devil's Food Rice Crispy Treats, 158
Dirt Cupcakes, 15
Dirt Doughnuts, 150
Double Chocolate Cupcakes Filled with Sweet Mascarpone, 8
Double Chocolate Peanut Butter Cupcakes, 20
Double Chocolate Peanut Butter Whoopie Pies, 145
Doughnuts
    Devil's food, 150
    dirt, 150
    red velvet, 162

E

Easy Berry Cobbler, 173
Eggnog Cookies, 119
Eggnog glaze, 119

F

Filling
    banana cream, 12
    brown sugar cream, 138
    cheesecake, 165
    cherry, 3
    chocolate peanut butter, 145
    coconut cream, 142
    cream cheese, 130, 133, 137, 141
    creamy coconut, 83
    German chocolate, 129
    green minty cream, 75
    lime mascarpone, 23
    mascarpone, 8
    peanut butter chocolate, 145
    pumpkin pie, 166
    raspberry whipped cream, 98
Food scoops, 182
Frequently asked questions, 188
Frosting
    cake batter, 16
    cookie dough, 80
    cream cheese, 11, 34, 59, 87
    cream cheese lime, 23
    graham cracker, 7
    lime cream cheese, 23
    peanut butter, 134
    peanut butter chocolate, 20
Frosting a cake, 186

G

Ganache, 91
    almond chocolate, 29
    chocolate, 3, 75, 158
    peanut butter, 20
German chocolate filling, 129
German Chocolate Whoopie Pies, 129
Glaze, 63, 162
    cherry, 55
    chocolate, 48, 52, 64, 150, 161
    cinnamon, 40
    cream cheese, 43, 56, 68
    eggnog, 119
    hot chocolate, 47
    lemon, 4, 51, 67
    maple, 44
    orange, 39, 71
Graham cracker crust, 27, 149
Graham cracker frosting, 7
Grasshopper cookies, 111
Green minty cream filling, 75

H

Haupia, 83
Hawaiian Vacation Cake, 83
Hot Chocolate Bundt Cake, 47
Hot chocolate glaze, 47
How to fill a piping bag, 180

K

Key Lime Cookie Bars, 165
Key Lime Pie Cookies, 120

L

Layers, making more, 185
Lemon Berry Cake, 95
Lemon Blueberry Poppy Seed Bundt Cake, 51
Lemon buttercream, 95
Lemon cake, 67, 95, 98
Lemon Cookies, 124
Lemon glaze, 4, 51, 67
Lemon Raspberry Whipped Cream Cake, 98

Lemonade cake, 4
Leveling cakes, 185
Lime coconut cupcakes, 23
Lime cookies, 120
Lime cream cheese frosting, 23
Lime curd, 120
Lime mascarpone filling, 23
Liners, cupcake, 179
Lining pans, 185

M

Mango pineapple cake, 83
Maple glaze, 44
Maraschino Cherry Cupcakes, 30
Mascarpone filling, 8
Mascarpone lime filling, 23
Mini Cherry Almond Bundts, 55
Mistakes with buttercream, 184
Mousse, white chocolate, 24

O

Oatmeal cookies, 138
Oatmeal Whoopie Pies, 138
Orange Cranberry Bundt Cake, 71
Orange cranberry cake, 71
Orange glaze, 39, 71

P

Pans, cake, which to use, 184
Pans, lining, 185
Peach cake, 56
Peaches and Cream Bundt Cake, 56
Peanut butter buttercream, 92
Peanut Butter Chocolate Chip Pumpkin Cookies, 103
Peanut butter chocolate filling, 145
Peanut butter chocolate frosting, 20

Peanut butter frosting, 134
Peanut butter ganache, 20
Peanut Butter Swirl Brownies, 169
Peanut butter swirl, 169
Peppermint Bark Cupcakes, 19
Peppermint white chocolate chunk buttercream, 19
Pineapple Cake with Sweet Strawberries, 60
Pineapple cake, 11
Pineapple Cream Cupcakes, 11
Pineapple mango cake, 83
Pineapple upside-down cake, 60
Piping bag, how to fill, 180–181
Piping tips, 179
Poppy seed lemon blueberry cake, 51
Pumpkin Bundt Cake, 59
Pumpkin cake, 59
Pumpkin chocolate chip cake cookies, 137
Pumpkin Chocolate Chip Whoopie Pies, 137
Pumpkin Pie Bars, 166
Pumpkin pie filling, 166
Puppy chow, red velvet, 153

Q

Questions, frequently asked, 188

R

Raspberry buttercream, 95
Raspberry cake, 43
Raspberry chocolate cake, 29
Raspberry Lemonade Bundt Cake, 67
Raspberry swirl, 67
Raspberry whipped cream filling, 98
Raspberry White Chocolate Bundt Cake, 43
Raspberry White Chocolate Mousse Cupcakes, 24

Red velvet brownies, 149
Red velvet cookies, 133
Red Velvet Doughnuts, 162
Red Velvet Puppy Chow, 153
Red Velvet S'mores Bars, 149
Red velvet strawberry cake, 34
Red Velvet Whoopie Pies, 133
Removing Bundt cakes from pan, 184
Rice crispy treats, 157, 158
Rocky Road Cake, 91
Round tops on cupcakes, how to get, 178

S

S'mores Cupcakes, 7
Scoops, food, 182
Snickerdoodle buttercream, 96
Snickerdoodle Cake, 96
Snickerdoodle Peanut Butter Whoopie Pies, 134
Snickerdoodles, 116, 134
Stacking cake layers, 186
Strawberries, sweet, 60
Strawberry buttercream, 88
Strawberry red velvet cake, 34
Strawberry Red Velvet Cupcakes, 34
Strawberry swirl, 64
Strawberry Vanilla Cake, 88
Streusel topping, 166
Substitution for cake mix, 176
Sweet potato cake, 27
Sweet Potato Pie Cupcakes with Brown Sugar Buttercream, 27
Sweet strawberries, 60
Swirl
    cake batter, 154
    cinnamon, 68
    peanut butter, 169
    raspberry, 67
    strawberry, 64

T

Tips, piping, 179
Topping
    streusel, 166
    whipped cream, 3
Trail mix cookies, 123

U

Ultimate Grasshopper Cookies, 111

V

Vanilla cake, 68, 88

W

Waffles, chocolate, 161
Whipped cream lemon raspberry cake, 98
Whipped cream raspberry filling, 98
Whipped cream topping, 3
White cake mix substitution, 176
White chocolate quick mousse, 24
White chocolate raspberry Bundt cake, 43
Whoopie pies
    brownie cream, 130
    carrot cake, 141
    chocolate coconut, 142
    chocolate peanut butter, 145
    German chocolate, 129
    oatmeal, 138
    pumpkin chocolate chip, 137
    red velvet, 133
    snickerdoodle peanut butter, 134

Y

Yellow cake, 63
Yellow sprinkle cake, 16

Z

Zucchini chocolate Bundt cake, 40